Can I Fax a Thank-You Note?

Can I Fax a Thank-You Note?

Audrey Glassman

BERKLEY BOOKS, NEW YORK

This book is an original publication of The Berkley Publishing Group.

CAN I FAX A THANK-YOU NOTE?

A Berkley Book / published by arrangement with
the author

PRINTING HISTORY
Berkley trade paperback edition / August 1998

The Penguin Putnam Inc. World Wide Web site address is
http://www.penguinputnam.com

ISBN: 0-425-16433-0

BERKLEY®
Berkley Books are published by The Berkley Publishing Group,
a member of Penguin Putnam Inc.,
200 Madison Avenue, New York, New York 10016.
BERKLEY and the "B" design
are trademarks belonging to Berkley Publishing Corporation.

PRINTED IN THE UNITED STATES OF AMERICA

10 9 8 7 6 5 4 3 2 1

In loving memory of my mother,
Judy Glassman,
whose kindness and wisdom continue to inspire.

Grateful acknowledgment and thanks to Danielle Claro, for tossing this book in my lap, for explaining why it belonged there, and for encouragement and editorial support along the way; Kathy Kleidermacher, for great ideas, flexibility, and gentle guidance; Jules Glassman, for yellow Post-its, legal-paper notes and "have you thought about . . ." conversations; my sisters, Ellen Gidaro and Beth Arnold, even though they say this book is proof that I'm their brother; Ms. Pamela Bicket, friend and reader extraordinare; Jennifer Kern, whose organizational skills, down to IIA3bi, astound me and saved me; Jacob Vernick, for being the kind of perfect baby boy who lets his mom write a book; and always, Michael Vernick, my technical consultant, baby-sitter, all-around expert, husband, and best friend.

Contents

Introduction — 1

Beep Me, Ring Me, Love Me — 5

Hullo? — 7

THE TELEPHONE — 9

TECHNO-FACTS: How Phones Work — 9

Telephone Etiquette:
Your Reputation's on the Line — 12

   Before You Dial — 12

   Everyone Deserves a Greeting — 13

   How to Talk on the Phone — 14

   Hold That Thought — 16

   When Answering Others' Phones — 18

   Ring Ring Ring Ring Ring — 20

   Leaving Messages — 21

   How Not to Be "It" — 24

   Response Time — 24

   *How to Record an Outgoing Greeting
Without Sounding Like a Goon* — 25

   When You'll Be Away — 26

   Timing Is Everything — 28

   Who Calls Back Whom? — 29

   Getting Off the Phone — 30

Oops, Wrong Number   31
I'm Calling to Tell You About a Very
    Special Offer . . .   32
**How to Avoid Certain Calls and Other
Useful Phone Services**   35
Call Waiting   36
Call Answering   37
Message-Delivery Service   38
Caller I.D.   38
Blocking/Anonymous Call Rejection   39
Call Return   41
Conference Calls   41
Screening Calls   43
Different Rules for Different Phones   45
Speaker Phones   45
Pay Phones   46
Video Phones   48
Special Rules for Home Businesses   48

CELLULAR TELEPHONES   51

**TECHNO-FACTS: How Cellular Phones
Work**   51
Cellular Phone Etiquette   52
Instrument of Last Resort   53
On the Receiving End   55
How to Talk on a Cellular Phone in
    Public   56
Be Prepared, Little Scout   56
Just Because Everyone Does It Doesn't
    Mean It's Right   57
Privacy and Security   59

WAS THAT YOURS OR MINE? 61

TECHNO-FACTS: How Beepers Work 61
   Beeper Etiquette 62

THE MANY TALENTS OF YOUR PHONE LINE 65

TECHNO-FACTS: How Modems and ISDNs Work 65
(Nothing But the) Fax 67
TECHNO-FACTS: How Fax Machines Work 67
   Neatness Counts! 68
   Cover Me 69
   Call Ahead? 69
   When Not to Fax 71

Online and Upward 73

OVERSIMPLIFIED INTRO TO COMPUTERS 75

TECHNO-FACTS: How Computers Work 75
   Other Nifty Computer Terms to Bandy About 79
   Modem or Fax/Modem? 80

E-MAIL BASICS 81

TECHNO-FACTS: How E-mail Works 81
   Before You Start 83
   E-mail Features 83
   A Subject Heading Is Worth a Thousand Words 85
   Signatures: Choose Your Handle with Care 86

E—MAIL ETIQUETTE   89

   Okay, Class. Let's Begin.   89
   Keep It Clean   90
   Response Time   91
   >Quote Back   93
   Word
   Wrap   93
   Don't Write Just to Write; It Ain't
    Right   94
   Excuse Me, That Was Private!   95
   Using E-mail to Avoid Confrontation   96
   Are We Friends or Business Associates?   97
   Only to Whom It May Concern   97
   Special Rules for Home Businesses   98
   Check It Twice   99
   Your Humor Is Lost on Me   100
   Smile When You Say That   101
   Abbrev.   103

OUT ON THE NET   107

Techno-Facts: How the Information
Superhighway Works   107
   What Intricate Webs We Weave!   109
   The Language of the Internet   111
   No, Thanks, I'm Just Browsing   111
   Your Very Own Web Page   113

**LET'S GO SURFING NOW, EVERYBODY'S
LEARNING HOW**   115

   I Got My Board, Now What Do I Do?   115
   Come On In, the Water's Great!   116
   Send Out a Search Party   117

VENTURING INTO THE CYBERWORLD — 121

Bulletin-Board Services — 121
Mailing Lists and Newsgroups — 122
Let's Start Near the Very Beginning (A Fairly Good Place to Start) — 124
Posting Your Brilliant Ideas — 125
Moderation or Saturation — 126
Chitchat — 127
How Lovely to Chat with You — 127
Webcasting — 129
Netiquette — 129
Mind Your Manners — 129
Spoiler Warnings — 132
The Nastiness Out There — 133
Spam, Spam, Spam — 135
Taking It to E-mail — 136
Play It Safe in Cyberspace — 137
The Politics of Passwords — 137
Use Your Noodle — 137
The Internet and Children — 138

WHEN TO DO WHAT — 141

What Are Your Options? — 141
Pros and Cons of Post and Calls — 142
Formal or Casual? — 145

TRAVELING WITH TECHNOLOGY — 149

Before You Travel — 149
Equipment for Your Equipment — 150
In the Car — 150
In the Airport — 151
In the Sky — 152

TECHNO—FAVORS   155

    Know the Rules   155
    Borrowing Equipment   157

HOW TO BE POLITE IN A RUDE WORLD   161

    Music That Moves (with) Us   161
    Handheld Electronic Games   162
    Things That Go Beep in the Night   163
    ATM (Avert, Then Move)   163
    Saving Marriages by Remote   164
    I Told You to Say Cheese!   165
    Know How to Work It   166

KEEP IT LEGAL   169

    It's Mine and You Can't See it   169
    But, Officer, I Didn't Know . . .   170
    Public Domain/Shmublic Shmomain   170

Glossary   173

Afterword   187

Can I Fax a Thank-You Note?

Introduction

It happens all the time. You're walking down the street, whistling a snappy tune, when suddenly you glance down and realize you're the only person on earth still wearing Frye boots; everyone else's feet are clad in smashing, stylish shoes, and you just forgot to notice. You tune in to *Saturday Night Live* at the beginning of each season, just knowing it's going to be great, only to find out that everyone else gave up more than a decade ago.

They've done it again. While you paused to gape at your metaphorical boot, they created a whole world of knowledge and acceptable behavior. They check their voice mail. They say "dot com." They surf, they chat, they multitask. They have profound insights into the lives of e-mail friends they've never met. Some of them know how to use equipment you didn't even know had been invented. They're smart, well rounded, and they never say, "How do I work this thing?"

Regardless of whether you have happily integrated modern technology into your life or are still standing on the sidelines, cheering halfheartedly, this book will help you become more knowledgeable and sophisticated in your daily techno-dealings. Maybe you already know how to use the technology of the moment and you need to brush up on your techno-etiquette. Perhaps you're pleased with the way the computer looks on your desk, with stacks of neat books piled next to it, and you're getting ready to think about turning it on. Or maybe you're one of those throwbacks who still hangs up on answering machines, gripped with fear at the thought of a circle of friends gathered around, replaying your awkward message repeatedly as they hold their bellies and howl with laughter.

Whether you think HTTP is the hallucinogenic drug of the moment or you're just not sure if it's okay to ask to borrow someone's cellular phone, the techno-world can sometimes seem like a place where near-human robots with glazed eyes press buttons and make things beep. There's a parallel universe out there with its own customs, strange abbreviations, and rules. There are questions you may feel it's too late to ask, lest you reveal to the world you're a techno-boob. This book will erase the confusion. It will demystify the complex web (if you will) of technology, help you acquire new skills, and make you more surefooted for your techno-journey. It will explain various technology in simple language that makes no assumptions about your techno-knowledge, other than basics, like electricity. (Special "Techno-Facts" sections, scattered throughout the text, will give you a tour of the nuts and bolts of various machines and technologies.) It will define everything from beepers to cellular phones, CD-ROMs to the Internet, and all the little things in between.

It will also provide insight into the etiquette of the technological world. In addition to learning the proper way to use the technology, you'll master the small, unspoken do's and don'ts for each. Even if you consider yourself a pro, you may want to check it out just to make sure you're the enlightened techno-cat you imagine yourself to be.

I hope when you have finished reading this book you will think about technology in a different way. Its mission, should you choose to accept it, is to make you aware of ideas you never even conceived of before, and help you be a more considerate, techno-savvy, intelligent person. You can also acquire perfect muscle tone, achieve nirvana, and get a shiny new convertible. But that part's up to you.

Beep Me, Ring Me, Love Me

Hullo?

We use the telephone like a bunch of buffoons. While it's clearly one of the simplest technologies to master (pick up, dial number, let ring, talk), it's where most people make the most mistakes on a daily basis.

Because we've been using telephones almost since we could speak, it's become an automatic-response technology. In other words, we forget to stop and think about what we're doing. Big deal, you may say. But think about it for a second. A potential customer calls an office and gets trapped in an endless hold loop by the call-answering technology. You leave a voice-mail message when applying for a job, but you forget to include vital information and you say "like, uh" three times. You put your client on speaker phone and fail to mention there are other people present, and your client happens to insult the fashion sense of one of those very people.

The telephone as communication tool has a lot to recommend it. If you're lucky and the person you're calling is available, it allows you the fastest connection. Both people talk in real time, business accomplished, budda-bing, budda-boom. Its downside, of course, is that of all communication vehicles, the telephone is the most intrusive. Its message is: I want to talk to you now, so be available to me regardless of what else you might be doing.

And it's getting more complicated all the time. Not that long ago, we dragged our index finger around the dials of our rotary phones and we hung up when the person we were calling was on another call or didn't answer. Now we leave messages; we reach someone who's already on the telephone; we press a button for temporary privacy from the person on the other end; we find out who's calling without even picking up the phone; we navigate menu systems and get the information we need with no human contact; we talk to more than one person at the same time. But do we do it politely?

Not without some thought. Let's face it—we screw up every day. The way to fix it is to think about it. The way to think about it is to read about it. Don't you love it when someone makes it simple for you to be the good person you know in your heart you really mean to be?

the Telephone

To truly understand the vast depths of your telephone, you must start from the inside. Technology is changing faster than books on the subject can be printed, but at its most basic, the way a telephone works goes a little something like this: Consider, if you will, that within a telephone system, there are two different communication links. The inside link is from your handset to your telephone base. The outside link is from your telephone base through the outside world to someone else's telephone. There are also two different ways a signal, such as a sound, can be transmitted–by analog or digital means.

When you transmit a signal, a pattern is created, and that pattern represents the message being sent. (Did I forget to warn you that during this explanation you might briefly experience a subtle nausea similar to the one you felt in high school physics? It will pass.) If you were to draw what an **analog** signal looks like, it would be comprised of continuous peaks and valleys of varying heights (picture the readout on a lie-detector machine on your favorite cop show). A **digital** system, on the other hand, is discontinuous and transmits only two specific values—0s and 1s, known as bits (picture a message sent in Morse code, with only dots and dashes). A **byte** is a series of eight bits.

In analog signals, different sounds produce different waves. Specifically, the difference will be reflected in the amplitude (distance between the peak and the valley) of the waves and their frequency (the number of times per second the cycle of the wave is repeated). These differences represent the specific qualities of a sound. For example, the greater the amplitude, the louder the sound will be.

On the digital side of things, everything is reduced into bits, those 0s and 1s. Instead of the waves being continuous and of widely varying heights, as in analog form, digital signals are discontinuous and either up or down, on or off. The more bytes used to represent a sound, the higher the quality of the sound.

Let's consider the difference between the two in real-world terms. Those of you old enough to remember vinyl records may also remember the first time you heard a compact disc (CD). The difference in sound quality was stunning. Why? Analog signals, that is, those on vinyl records, can degrade and get fuzzy over time. When tiny particles get in the way of a phonograph needle going up and down on your REO Speedwagon album, you hear it, and it changes the sound. Likewise, over long distances, the quality of sound, transmitted by analog signals, can degrade. There are infinite values within an analog signal, which means even the slightest deviation causes distortion. But a CD, because it is digital, has less room for error. Even if there were some degradation in the value of one of those 0s or 1s, there would still be only two distinct values, which makes it almost impossible for the same kind of distortion to degrade the sound. That's why a compact disc sounds so clear and pure.

Got it? Analog is based on waves and their inherent amplitude and frequency. Digital is based on series of 0s and 1s. While this may sound too abstract to actually get your brain around, you now know enough.

Getting back to phones...

Those links we were talking about, the inside link and outside link, can be either analog or digital. With POTS (plain old telephone service), the outside link is analog. That means when you're talking on an analog phone, the sound of your voice is changed into an electric current at the handset, sent over the inside link, through your phone, through the outside link, and into the inside link of the phone of the person you're calling, where it is converted back into sound waves at that person's handset. (An awful lot of work just to say hi.) When you're talking on a digital phone, the handset translates your sound waves into a digital signal which is sent to the base station and converted into an analog signal before being sent to the outside link.

Phones with cords (and wired inside links) are always analog. Cordless phones have wireless inside links and can be either analog or digital. Digital provides a clearer connection because it is less prone to interference and distortion. In fact, some digital phones allow almost a mile of distance between telephone and handset, so you can stay connected even when you take your dog for a walk.

Telephone Etiquette:
Your Reputation's on the Line

How do you want to be perceived? Accurately, perhaps. Or if you believe yourself to be a bit of an idiot, maybe you'd like to be perceived as a better person than you actually are. Fortunately, you are not what you eat, or what you wear; to the majority of people you interact with, you are what you say on the phone.

There's more to talking on the phone than dialing, talking, and hanging up. There are simple things you can do and say that will reveal to the world the wonderful, wise, and considerate person you really are.

BEFORE YOU DIAL

Before you use a new telephone or a new phone service, you should understand how to use it properly. This should go without saying, but so should a lot of things that still need saying.

There's an expression out there in the techno-world that may have a bit of profanity in it, but it rings true: RTFM. It stands for "read the manual," with a modifying adjective that begins with the letter f. Maybe it's *funny*, maybe *fantastic*, maybe something else. In any event, it's good advice. The materials may be dry and dull but they will give you the information you need if you want to use your phone properly. And you do. You may think exceptions should be made for someone like you. You may be wrong. The worst offenses are the ones in which the offenders should know better: accidental telephone disconnections, receiving twenty-five blank pages on your fax—you get the picture.

Make it your personal telephone policy never to use lame equipment. If your cordless telephone has interference from one of your neighbor's appliances and you hear a constant static crackle, don't use it. If you lose more messages than you get, don't turn on your machine—fix it, or buy a new one. And if you have a phone that sometimes cuts off calls unexpectedly, get rid of it.

EVERYONE DESERVES A GREETING

Have you noticed how impolite people are on the phone? You sweetly answer your phone: "Hello?" You're greeted with "Yeah. Let me talk to Billy," or "Uh, I was callin' about the tickets," or "Is Sherry there?"

The person answering your phone call at the very least deserves a hello. If you are acquainted with the person answering the phone—even if you just know his name or have only spoken with him on the phone—you should try to greet him with a sentence. This is equally important in social and business situations. Say you're calling your friend Liz and her husband, George, answers the phone. Depending on how close you are with George, you may say, "Hi, George, it's (your name). How are you?" or something like that. It is rude simply to say, "Hi George, it's (your name), can I speak to Liz?" George deserves a polite social interchange.

That's the rule. Here's the exception: George is a world-renowned curmudgeon. Of course, world-renowned curmudgeons should not answer the phone, but that's George's problem. If you know the person you're talking to hates small talk, hates all talk, or hates you, just get yourself connected to whomever you need to speak to, in whatever way you want.

Likewise, in a business setting, people who answer phones should be greeted. Understandably, many of them are dealing with busy phone lines or switchboards and cannot be bothered, but they are sure to appreciate the effort, and you'll be able to get a sense of how responsive they are to a cheerful "Hi, Mr. Brisbane, it's (your first and last name) from (your business affiliation). How are you today?" Being polite takes minimal effort, and can foster a friendly relationship between you and the person who answers the telephone. In addition to making that telephone answerer feel acknowledged as a person—as opposed to a human voice-mail mechanism—it has the added benefit of putting you on the good side of someone close to a person with whom you work. (And you don't need to be told how important that can be.)

HOW TO TALK ON THE PHONE

There are no rules governing banter and friendly back-and-forth on the phone. Different people have different comfort zones for such things. You can judge on a case-by-case basis how much interest your business colleagues, clients, and superiors have in small talk. But there is always a proper place to start: Identify yourself. The "guess who this is" game is never fun.

How do you introduce yourself? In most social situations, a first name is sufficient, unless your name is Michael, John, Mary, or something that was once one of the ten most popular boys' or girls' names in a given year. If it's a social call to someone whom you never or rarely call, you should specify the context, as in, "Hi, it's Nils from the softball team." In business situations, unless you are speaking to someone with whom you speak on a daily basis, you should always say your first and last name as well as your business affiliation. If you work for a large corporation, that might go for interoffice calls, too.

It's also important to make an effort to speak clearly. Think about how frustrating it is to have to say, "What? What? I'm sorry, what did you say? *What?*" If you are known as a fast talker (in the literal sense), make a concerted effort to slow down. You may be understood by your friends and colleagues in person, but over the phone, they lose the benefit of their visual read—your lips moving—and have to rely on their ears.

Before you receive an expected call or place one yourself, think of everything you mean to say and jot it down. You don't need a script, but notes can be helpful. Look at your list before you hang up. If, in your phone history, you frequently find yourself saying, "Hi. It's me again. I forgot one thing," it would be a good idea to organize your thoughts in detail on paper very thoroughly before you get on the phone.

And don't do dumb things while you're on the phone. Dumb

things include: talking to someone else who happens to be in the room (if you must, excuse yourself first), chewing gum, watching a game show, eating anything, glancing over the day's headlines, and playing computer games.

HOLD THAT THOUGHT

The hold button has always been one of the most hated telephone technologies (Call Waiting bumped it out of the top spot a few years ago). But it does serve an important function. In business situations in particular, it is a vital tool for a phone answerer with more than one line. But for how long is it okay to put someone on hold?

To start, a bit of almost-but-not-quite-yet-archaic telephone etiquette: Don't just *tell* someone you're putting him on hold. Rather, you should *ask* him if you can. Of course, most people are programmed to say yes. But there are those people out there who are not like you and me. They may answer, "No, you may not, young man," or worse. It's best to weed out the people who are dreadfully offended by the concept of hold and prevent further insult. In that situation, you can either handle the call, or take a message and return the call at a more convenient time.

Other than that, there is no clear standard of acceptability here: Different people have different hold thresholds. If you are going to put someone on hold for more than a minute, you should inform her and give her the choice of leaving a message or calling back later. It's her dime and her time, and she should have the option of choosing how to proceed.

Once you are in the midst of a conversation with someone, it is not polite to ask him to hold. Of course, this creates enormous problems for those with Call Waiting service. If you know there may be Call Waiting interruptions while you're talking to someone, inform him at the outset. You're still being rude, but at least your cards are on the table.

In the rare instance when you know in advance that you will need to put someone on hold—or hang up on her if someone else calls or your appointment shows up—she deserves to be told in advance and to decide whether or not she wishes to proceed with the call. As an example, one of your clients phones five minutes before your boss is supposed to call from the road. You can simply not take the call and call the client back at a more convenient time, or you can explain the situation and let the client make the choice. It's only fair. Because if you start talking, you know your boss will call on time, even though she never has before.

If you do put someone on hold and you can see that it's going to take longer than a minute, you must get back to that caller and inform him, politely asking whether he would like you to get back to him within the next (specify time accurately), or whether he'd like to continue to hold for another (specify time honestly).

Of course, it would be nice if we could always behave considerately in the course of everyday business; whenever possible, these guidelines should be followed. But in the real world, there are going to be a lot of exceptions to this and just about every rule. Your goal is to be impolite and/or unprofessional as infrequently as possible.

There will be very important calls that come into your office while you're on less important calls. What's a person to do? If you're lucky enough to have an assistant who understands which calls are important and which aren't, and one who doesn't mind standing and walking a little bit, maybe he stands in the doorway of your office with one of those "there's another call" looks or sneaks a note in front of you while you're on the phone to inform you of the second call. It's certainly more polite than a voice breaking in on the intercom. You can say, "Please excuse me for a second, Joyce," without further explanation, as he tells you who is on the other line or while you read the note. And if you need to take the other call, a simple apology and agreement of when to resume the conversation should suffice. In most cases it's a good idea not to say, "Joyce? Listen, I'll have to get back to you around four. Ramsey's calling and I have to speak with him." Think about the impression that gives Joyce: He's preempting *my* call? What's so sacred about Ramsey?!

What about when *you're* stuck on hold? While it might seem rude, it is perfectly acceptable to hang up if someone has put you on hold for more than a couple of minutes without an explanation. There is rudeness involved here, but it's not yours.

WHEN ANSWERING OTHERS' PHONES

In an office environment, there are many different situations in which someone could be called upon to answer another person's phone. Of course, receptionists do it all day. But in many offices, receptionists also go to lunch, and other arrangements for answering the phone are made. In some offices, this is not a problem. In others, it is the single greatest contributing factor to embittered, disgruntled employees. And that bitter attitude is, of course, passed along to innocent callers.

In an office, people who answer the phone should be friendly, or at the very least efficient. Every employee in a company should know how to answer the phone without sounding resentful and sullen. This may be your office's initial contact with a client— you want to make a favorable impression. In fact, it's not a bad idea for employers to call their own companies at different times of the day to monitor how their phone-answering employees are doing. Is your best foot being put forward—or directly placed into someone's mouth?

The rules of phone answering are also significant for companies that do not have human receptionists. Let's say you're sitting in Ralph's office and he's stepped out to the copier. His phone rings. His voice mail does not pick up. Unless Ralph has wacky rules about his phone, you would be doing the right thing by answering his phone and informing the caller that someone other than Ralph is doing the answering. Something like "Ralph Malph's office, this is (your first and last name). May I help you?"

This may come up in personal situations, too. You're at Max's house and he has to go next door to borrow some paper clips. Of course, his phone rings while he's out and no one else is home. If he has a machine, you should let it do the answering unless Max specifically directed you to answer his phone. How to proceed in the absence of a machine is a matter of personal preference and depends on the nature of the relationship. Many people would rather stick their tongue to dry ice than answer a phone in someone else's home. But if you do decide to answer it, it would be best not to just say "Hello?" but something more like "(Max's last name) residence." While this may make you feel like Alice on *The Brady Bunch,* it will inform the caller that someone other than Max or his immediate family is answering the phone, so the caller is less apt to, say, sing "Happy Birthday" to you or offer throaty, sexy reminiscences of last night.

RING RING RING RING RING

Answering machines and most voice-mail and voice-answering services allow you to choose the number of times your phone will ring before the technology kicks in. Some machines can save you the cost of calling in for messages by ringing more times, say four, if there are no new messages, and fewer, say twice, if there are. Excepting that, if you turn your machine on only when you're out, there's no good reason to have your phone ring more than once before your greeting plays. Some callers may complain that this doesn't give them a chance to hang up before the machine picks up, but most machines won't even record a hang-up if the caller disconnects before the completion of the greeting.

Maybe you have a call-answering service that picks up automatically if you don't answer the phone after a set number of rings. If you don't spend a lot of time near your phone, and you find yourself racing through the living room, dining room, and kitchen to answer in time, you should give yourself enough ring time to reach the phone. Sure, people may be annoyed at the long wait to leave a message when you don't pick up, but no one's twisting their arms here. They can hang up when they want.

If you let your phone ring too many times before the machine or service answers, you run the risk of not receiving messages from callers who don't know you and assume there is no machine. Four rings is the generally accepted standard. Consider your needs and your callers' needs—and select your ring setting accordingly.

LEAVING MESSAGES

What are the important elements of a message? Who called, and what she wants. Sometimes the time she called might be important, too. So why is it that people don't know how to do this? When you place a call, you should be equally prepared to speak to the person or to leave a message.

When leaving a message the old-fashioned way—with a person, as in a receptionist, assistant, family member, or roommate—give all the information the person you're calling will need. When someone asks, "And your number, please," do not say, "He has it." If you've ever received a written phone message, you know how much easier it is to call the person back when the phone number is right there in good old black and white. Even if the person you're calling knows your phone number by heart, his assistant may very well have been instructed to obtain callers' numbers no matter what. Make their lives easier—just give it up.

When you're leaving a message on an answering machine or voice-mail service, the equation is about the same, except the machine can't say, "Excuse me, I didn't make out the last thing you said." So speak slowly. "Hi Lucy. It's Ricky. I'm at the club, 555-4444. Please call me back."

In business situations, you need to be more specific. If you're calling Dan and he's a really busy, happening guy, a message that says "Hey, it's me. Call me back" doesn't do him a lot of good. Do you want to offer Dan a free box of cigars, throw some business his way, or complain that he still hasn't paid you back for that dinner three weeks ago? Dan may need to prioritize his calls, and your less-than-informative message gives him no way to do that. Your message would be fine if you were just calling Dan to chat, like you always do. But if you're doing something other than calling a friend to shoot the breeze, you should briefly mention why you're calling. This is especially true for personal messages if that information would reveal some time-relevant context, as in "I have an extra ticket for tonight's monster truck rally. Wanna go?"

If your message is longer than two sentences, repeat your name and phone number at the very end. But don't ramble. If the voice-mail service offers the option to listen to the message you have just left, do it. *Really* listen to it. If it rambles, sounds too fast, or contains anything like "Oh, wait, I just remembered," erase it and start again.

You do not want to become known as an obnoxious message leaver. There are a number of ways to achieve this distinction, and they should all be avoided like the p-l-a-g-u-e. For starters, do not leave obnoxious messages, like "Remember me?" You should also be aware of the number of messages you leave. Some inconsiderate, impatient callers leave a message and call back within the hour if they have not heard back. And make sure not to use the word *urgent* too liberally. Consider yourself forewarned:

A lot of folks are apt to put the messages of the obnoxious at the bottom of their to-do pile.

With all messages, if you know you are going to be out from noon until two, say so—or, better yet, tell the person you're calling the ideal time at which she can return your call. (For many people, however, this can lead to "If you want to call before lunch, call me at the office. If you need to reach me between 11:30 and 12:45, though, I'll be in the car, so call that phone. I'll be in a meeting in the afternoon, so call my beeper and I'll call you back." Not a great plan. The best advice is to keep it as brief as possible, but to convey the information needed to connect.)

If you are someone, like a salesman, whose business relies on leaving messages and having people get back to you, you should make an even greater effort to sound professional and respectable. It sounds goofy, but it's even a good idea to audiotape-record yourself as you leave messages, just to get a really good read on it. Listen to yourself critically; would *you* buy from you?

Leaving a message does not take a lot of time. Take the time to do it right. Do not be in the midst of blowing the world's best bubble-gum bubble while you're reciting your name and phone number.

Be aware that there will be times in your long life when the smart thing to do is *not* to leave a message. Say you were calling to see if your friend just saw that video on VH1 that was filmed near your apartment and sort of shows the front of your car, kind of, but he's not home, so he probably didn't see it. It won't make for the most compelling message, will it?

HOW NOT TO BE "IT"

Phone tag isn't fun. It's time-consuming, frustrating, and almost always inspires one of the participants to make a really lame joke. It can be avoided, and shrewd phone users know how.

The best way to eliminate phone tag, especially when you're dealing with someone's voice mail, is to leave a detailed message (as long as it's not too lengthy). Let's say you're calling Rosie to find out what time the meeting is next Thursday, and you reach Rosie's voice mail. Don't just leave your name and number; let her know exactly why you're calling and tell her she can leave a message on your voice mail. If she does, mission accomplished— no need to speak to anyone ever again! Likewise, when you get a message that seeks specific information, don't just say "returning your call" when you leave *your* message. Unless you are dealing with something of a confidential nature, leave the information, eliminate the need for more phone tag, and improve the universe!

If you do find yourself stuck in an endless phone-tag cycle, a valiant approach is to offer to be "it." Say you've been trying to reach Min for four days, and it's been a series of call-me-back messages on both ends. Instead of putting the ball back in Min's court, find out from a real-live person at Min's office what time would be best to reach her, and place the call again at the appropriate time. If Min remembers her playground rules, she'll know that next time around, she's it, no backsies.

RESPONSE TIME

In business situations, it is most professional to return calls within the same business day when possible, but at least within twenty-four hours. If you know you will be unable to contact someone by phone within twenty-four hours, it's a good idea to let him know that. Sometimes you can dash off an e-mail message to that effect. Or you can have someone from your office call the person and inform him of your situation, and let him know when he can expect to hear from you. Unless, of course, you're a lawyer, in which case no rules of courtesy apply.

In your personal life, the relationship tends to dictate the response time. If you have a friend with whom you generally speak once a month, it would not be unusual or impolite to wait a few days before returning the call, unless, of course, the message states some urgency. But if you speak to your brother a few times each day, it could be a sign of filial hostility to let even a day pass before calling.

HOW TO RECORD AN OUTGOING GREETING WITHOUT SOUNDING LIKE A GOON

Answering machines and other call-answering technology have been around long enough for people to know how they work. In other words, you no longer have to say "after the beep." One exception: If you happen to have one of those weird time-lapse, extra-long, or otherwise out-of-the-ordinary beeps on your machine, you may issue a brief warning to that effect—but a better solution would be to fix your beep.

When you record your message, do not use the outgoing message voice that lies on your surface; dig deeper into your soul. Talk the way you talk to your friends or colleagues, in that slow, relaxed voice. Don't yell. Some people suggest smiling while you leave your message to convey the happy-go-lucky person you really are. Try it; it may work. Or it may make you sound like a happy-go-lucky goon.

Since you're the one leaving the greeting, you get to set the tone. Tell callers what information you expect from them. Maybe the time they called is very important, but if you don't care, don't request it. If you want to cut down on phone tag, ask callers to leave the best time to reach them. That also gives them a greater sense of responsibility to take your call if you do call back at the specified time, even if they're in the midst of something else.

Keep your outgoing message brief. As cute or cool as it may seem to you, callers may not want to first hear your kitty mewing or your favorite song from that K-Tel record you just found. They may be calling from American Samoa, and your cleverness may cost them. Of course, it's your machine, you can cry if you want to—but try to keep it brief.

WHEN YOU'LL BE AWAY

If you know you won't be getting to your messages for a while, say so in a way that won't invite robbers to your house. For example, if you just brought home your new baby from the hospital, and talking on the phone is about forty-fifth on the list of things you intend to do in the next two weeks, say so. In this situation, you can also save yourself return calls by including the information people are seeking. "It's a girl named Starchild, born on the fourth. We're all doing well. We're sorry, but we won't get to our calls for a few days." Of course, if you're expecting calls from prospective employers or clients on the same line, this might not be the best strategy.

If it's a work voice-mail situation, try to give the caller a sense of how long it might take to hear back from you. For example, if your voice mail kicks in whether you're on the phone or away from your desk, say so. "This is (you). I'm in the office today, but away from my desk or on another line . . ." If you're in Houston for three days and know you won't get to your messages, don't forget to change your greeting. "I'm out of town and will return to the office on _____. If this is an emergency, you can reach my assistant at _____." When you change your regular greeting to an *I'm out of town* greeting, it's a good idea to dial your own number and leave a message reminding yourself to rerecord your greeting upon your return.

If there are people with whom you expect to speak while you're away on business, it is good form to get your vital communication statistics into their hands before your departure. Rather than having them call your office only to have a coworker inform them, "Oh, he's at the Hilton in Florida," do the footwork yourself. Call ahead to the hotel at which you will be staying for its fax number. Find out if the rooms have modem capabilities. If you discover you won't easily be able to access your e-mail, tell the people with whom you expect to communicate that the best way to reach you while you're away is by phone.

Keep in mind, too, that you're away from your phone not only when you go out of town, but for a good chunk of each day. Especially in the close quarters of apartment and dorm life, consider what that means for your neighbors. Turn down the volume on your machine so that when you're not home, your neighbors don't have to listen to a broadcast of your messages.

TIMING IS EVERYTHING

The telephone rings whenever it wants, or so it seems, and we are expected to answer. In business settings, for the most part, this is good news. It rings—more business! Sure, there are the difficulties of juggling calls and screening calls, but for most, it's our primary tool. There are, however, ways to play considerately with our tools and ways to play not so considerately. If you have to return a call to someone to whom you do not wish to speak, would you call when he is apt to be at lunch? Possibly. But you know what? Unless the person is really clueless (and he could be—maybe that's why you didn't want to speak to him in the first place), he'll know you did that on purpose.

And what about waiting until after business hours to return calls? The voice-mail seeker is not tricking anyone. He is calling when you won't be there because it's easier for him not to speak to you. But a number of return calls are about providing information, not about chatting. Let's say Sandy has been in meetings from ten to five-thirty. She gets back to her desk and finds a thick stack of pink messages or twenty minutes' worth of voice-mail messages. *Argh!* She picks up the phone and cranks out ten return voice-mail messages in as many minutes. It may not be the absolute greatest method of communication, but it's better than waiting a couple of days, especially if she offers a brief admission that she's aware of what she's doing: "I'm sorry to be calling at a time

I knew you wouldn't be there . . ." She should also specify a time at which she and the other party can plan to talk if the message she's leaving cannot supply sufficient information.

There are times when off-hours calls and/or faxes are perfectly acceptable. If you do some work at home and want to have a report on your client's desk in the morning, you can send it to his office in the evening. But the rules are different if your client has a home office. For many, that means a fax machine on a table right outside the nursery, or a computer on the kitchen table. If you have not made prior arrangements about off-hour calls, assume it would be disruptive to a home business.

What about getting in touch with people who are impossible to reach? Let's say you've been trying to get your friend Mabel on the phone for the past five days. You know she's always home at 6 P.M., because that's when she has dinner with her family. And let's say you really need to talk to her. No. You cannot call her at dinnertime. It's rude. What to do? When you have friends or colleagues who are difficult to contact, ask *them* how to proceed. Maybe they schedule all their phone time for the morning. Could be they're terrible with phone messages but scrupulous about their e-mail. The best way to communicate with those who are hard to reach is to have them commit to a very specific time and/or mode in advance.

WHO CALLS BACK WHOM?

There are times when telephone calls get cut off. This is usually followed by at least five minutes of trying to call each other and listening to each other's busy signals and/or voice-mail recordings.

Disconnections are usually someone's fault. Robin's two-year-old loves to pull the cord out of the wall while her mom's on the phone. When you get cut off, Robin should call you back. Leo's phone sometimes disconnects spontaneously. Leo has to initiate the return call. Of course, Robin should not allow her daughter to do that and Leo should buy a new phone, but until that happens, you can sit by your phone and wait.

Sometimes a disconnection is inexplicable, or at least you have no idea why it happened. In the case of a long-distance call, it is good form for the one who did not place the first call to initiate the second. On a plain old local phone call, on the other hand, the initial caller should place the second call.

GETTING OFF THE PHONE

Hear this: It is unacceptable to say, "I'll let you go now," when you want to end a telephone conversation. It is condescending and false. Let's say you've been on the phone with Robert for what feels like three hours. Clearly, Robert still feels like chatting, but your bladder and perhaps even your brain simply can't handle much more. If you utter those awful five words, you are pretending to offer him something he wants when in fact you are doing the opposite. You are making him feel responsible for something for which *you* should feel responsible. It's just plain rude.

So what do you do? You can apologize and tell Robert you've enjoyed talking to him, but you have to go, or say, "Gee, Robert, I wish I had more time to talk." Or you can lie: "Listen, Robert, I gotta go. There's an elephant in my backyard."

OOPS, WRONG NUMBER

Even the most careful among us have occasion to dial the wrong number. When you realize your mistake, don't just hang up. You should apologize. "Oh, I'm sorry. I dialed the wrong number." Simple. You do not need to know what number you actually reached; what good is that going to do you? If you reach the same number more than once, you can ask, "Is this 555-3902?" and then figure out wherein your mistake lies.

How about when you're the wrong number someone dialed? No need to be hostile here, folks. Just let the caller know he has reached the wrong number. If he tells you the number he's trying to reach, you can tell him if, in fact, that's the right number with the wrong person. You do not have any obligation beyond this, like hearing about the problems the caller has had reaching his Aunt Gertrude.

Wrong numbers aren't always simple. Modern technology has introduced modern conundrums: What's a guy to do when his wrong number results in a connection to a stranger's answering machine? It's best to hang up before the beep (during the greeting). Imagine Roger's disappointment when he returns home to the first message he's received in five weeks: "Sorry, wrong number."

Then, of course, there is also the problem of receiving a message from someone who did not realize she had reached the wrong machine. An important or urgent message left in the wrong place can spell disaster: "I found your three lost dogs." "The trial was moved up to tomorrow morning at 9 A.M." "Mom's on the roof." In these situations, even though the error was not yours, even if you're not usually a nice person, basic human decency dictates the necessity of informing the caller that she reached the wrong machine. Of course, if she didn't leave a number, you'll just have to be haunted by the situation for many sleepless nights. (Or, if circumstances and technology permit, you can try using call-return service.) For a misplaced *just called to say hi* message, you don't need to track down the caller to inform him of his mistake.

I'M CALLING TO TELL YOU ABOUT A VERY SPECIAL OFFER...

Finally, a moment alone with your life partner. Wine is chilled, tall, tapered candles flicker, extraordinary fragrances waft in from the kitchen. Phone rings. You answer. Very long pause. "Congratulations! You have been selected to receive a free in-home test of your tap water. That's right, a test in your home for free, with absolutely no obligation for future purchase."

The only thing more annoying than picking up the phone and hearing a telemarketer's voice asking you to buy something is picking it up to hear a machine voice asking you to buy something or, worse yet, to hear a machine ask you to hold to talk to an operator you never even wanted to talk to in the first place!

It is very tempting to create a whole different category of phone etiquette regarding telemarketing phone calls, with special rules that emphasize nastiness. But keep this in mind: Just because someone has chosen to make a living by calling you at inconvenient times of day to discuss something that is probably of no interest to you does not give you license to be vile. At least not right off the bat. (But feel free to try out any new or old favorite expletives on the recorded telemarketing voices that call your home.)

Unfortunately, common courtesy prevents us from behaving like the inner monsters we long to unleash when we receive unsolicited phone calls from strangers. There are a number of polite ways of getting off the phone with a telemarketer—you can choose the one that best suits your personality. There are also some less-than-nice ideas; all politeness and no rudeness makes Jill a dull girl.

The telemarketers' plan, of course, is to try to keep you on the phone as long as possible. The more you hear about their wonderful product or service, their theory goes, the more apt you are to give in and try it. Often, the pitch will begin with something like "Hello, Ms. (your name), this is Juniper Jones from the Three-way Area Restoration Center and I'm calling today to talk to you for just a minute about a wonderful new offer. How are you today, ma'am?" [Pause long enough for less-than-a-syllable response.] "That's great, ma'am, as I was saying, the reason I'm calling you today . . . ", and on it goes.

You can try to pipe in about your lack of interest during that pause, but chances are she won't let you. And bear in mind that the script she's following is written in such a way as to make it next to impossible for you to politely excuse yourself from this conversation that you never asked to take part in. So, at the first opportunity—or before it—you can respond, "I'm sorry, but I do not respond to phone solicitations." Many Juniper Joneses will just hang up. True, *they're* being rude, but at least you don't have to talk to them anymore.

A variation on that approach is to use Juniper's tricks back on her, saying something like "Actually, Juniper, we're one of those families that does not respond to telephone solicitations." The beauty of this approach is that Juniper Jones is apt to be temporarily stunned by the use of her name. Telemarketers, even though they are talking to people all day, are actually involved in a very dehumanized experience. You can use her moment of shock to say, "Thanks anyway," and hang up.

Now, if Juniper Jones is a bit more savvy, she's going to make this even harder for you. She may begin the call by asking, "Hello, is this [your name]?" or "Hello, may I speak to Ms. [your name]?" This leaves you in the unenviable position of either having to deny your identity or engaging in a dialogue with a stranger. But the rule is: You never have to talk to someone on the phone when you don't want to (with the possible exception of in-laws).

The most traditional response is to wait until the first available scripted pause and say, "I'm sorry. I'm not interested." It's their job to continue, but you've done your piece. You can begin the process of returning the phone to its cradle as you express your lack of interest, so you don't have to hear the rest of the plea.

Here's a technique some hardened solicitor-stomping veterans swear by. At your earliest possible response time, say, "You see that paper in front of you? You see that square that says 'never call back'? Please check that now."

You can ask to have your name removed from the calling lists of the companies that seek your business. The company is required by law to do so, but there's a good chance they'll say they will and in fact won't. If you are someone who is bombarded by calls, you can try to exasperate the caller by saying something like "Can you hold on a sec?" and putting the phone down. Of course, the caller will wait a while and then catch on to you, hang up, and move down to the next name on his list. Maybe you can derive some joy from annoying the callers who annoy you. It's not nice, but neither is receiving a call in the middle of a family meal.

Perhaps the only way to have a modicum of fun with telemarketers is to turn their calls into a game. Assuming, of course, that you are *not* interested in whatever they're peddling, you can try to think of the fastest way to get the person to hang up on *you*. When the bulk-meat-order people come calling, discuss your family's vegetarian lifestyle in detail and try to get the telemarketer to consider the health benefits of giving up beef. Or let's say it's an investment broker. You could try "Actually, I just filed for bankruptcy, but I'm really very interested in what you're offering. Could you please tell me more?"

How to Avoid Certain Calls and Other Useful Phone Services

There's a whole bevy of services that different phone companies offer, and some are more appealing than others. Even if you pride yourself on your stripped-down phone service, you should know about the services that are available, since many of the people who call you and whom you call are bound to use them. And one day, that special introductory rate might really tempt you to sign on for some yourself.

CALL WAITING

Call Waiting, known to some as *callus interruptus*, is a service that allows you to receive a phone call even when you're already talking to someone on the phone. A beep or series of beeps informs you that there is another call. The person to whom you are talking will not hear the beeps, and may or may not hear a tiny glitch in the connection. Call Waiting allows you to go back and forth between the calls, usually by pressing the switch hook or disconnect button.

More than almost any other modern invention, the concept of Call Waiting is a people divider. Despite its prevalence, it seems that most people find it the technological epitome of rudeness. In fact, it is one of the rare instances in which technology itself, and not the people using it, is blamed for poor manners.

Of course, there are many people out there who choose to have and pay for Call Waiting service. There are a variety of ways of classifying people who like Call Waiting. Some maintain it's an urban thing—the expectation that someone should wait while you check out what else is going on. This next one might be a bit of a stretch, but there's a case to be made that Call Waiting is the ultimate litmus test for the commitment-phobic—a sure sign of someone who is always convinced the better man or woman is out there. (Note good example of subsets here: Not all who have Call Waiting would be described as commitment-phobic, but most who are commitment-phobic could be expected to have Call Waiting.) Some, primarily parents, insist that they need to be reached in case of an emergency—what if they're on the phone chatting about the likelihood of a Bay City Rollers reunion tour when little Joey breaks his leg? (Apparently these people have never heard of having an operator make an emergency break in on their phone line.)

Since many people continue to use the service, it's worth reviewing the least impolite way to interrupt your phone conversations. When the Call Waiting signal sounds, let the person to whom you are talking know that you have another call and politely ask her if she would please hold on for a minute. The key to doing this in the least insulting way is to wait until *you're* talking and then interrupt *yourself*. Answer the other call, and find out who is calling and where and when you can reach him. If you are tempted to talk to the second caller, you should ignore the temptation; that is exactly why people hate Call Waiting. Think about how you feel when you're in the middle of a conversation and a Call Waiting call bumps you out of conversation rank. Except in the rare case of true emergency, a first call must maintain priority.

CALL ANSWERING

Many phone companies offer an alternative to Call Waiting, known as Call Answering, which will take a message if your phone rings more than a predetermined number of times or if you are on another call. To find out if you have messages, you have to pick up the phone to hear whether or not your dial tone has an interrupted beep. If it does, you place a call to a voice-messaging service to retrieve your messages.

While Call Answering is vastly less rude than Call Waiting, it does have its downside. For the most part, those who call you want to talk to you—not your machine, not your voice mail. Listening to your message when you're on the phone and when you're not home is bound to get annoying for those who call you, especially if you're on the phone and/or not home often. Also, the service can have the surprise effect of running up your phone bill as you will be expected to call back those who left messages while you were chatting. You may also be charged each time you call your voice-messaging service to retrieve your messages, depending upon the level of service you get from your local phone company. (If all this sounds too unpleasant, there's this old relic called a busy signal which people used to hear when they called your phone and the line was already in use.)

MESSAGE-DELIVERY SERVICE

Call Answering has a cousin service that is available to the person *placing* the call. Some phone companies offer a message-delivery service that allows you to leave a message when no human or machine answers the number you're calling, or even if you get a busy signal. If this service is available, you'll be prompted by a recorded instruction of what to do. Once you have recorded a message, the phone company will ring the phone periodically for a fixed amount of time and attempt to deliver your message. If the prompt fails to mention it, you may want to check how much you might be charged for using this service.

CALLER I.D.

Caller I.D. is a service that gives you information about a caller before you even answer the phone. (Just think of all the scary baby-sitter movies we would have been spared had this service been around years ago.) Depending on your area, your Caller I.D. box could display any of the following: the telephone number, the name, the date, and the time of the incoming call.

Caller I.D. has single-handedly diminished the frequency of a pervasive tele-nuisance. Yes, in a rare turn of events, technology has come up with a way to *prevent* rudeness. For a long time, there was a rash of rude behavior by the dreaded answering-machine seekers. People scheduled their calls for those times of days when the person they were calling was not apt to be home, wanting only to reach her machine—not the person herself. Sometimes these callers were surprised to have the person, not the machine, answer, and these awful people would just hang up. It was so easy then.

But now with the realization that the person they're trying to reach can figure out it was them with a simple glance at the Caller I.D. box to see who called—folks are less apt to hang up on their "friends." Of course, this doesn't really keep them from calling at times when they hope to get the machine, not the person, but at least it's not so easy to deny a hang-up anymore. Caller I.D. has the additional bonus of keeping down the number of crank calls a person can expect to receive in a lifetime.

BLOCKING/ANONYMOUS CALL REJECTION

Because you are still entitled to your privacy, there is a service that allows you to block identifying information. Per-call blocking temporarily conceals your phone number on any given call. To use it, you enter a code, after which you hear a dial tone that signals you to dial the number you're calling. Per-line blocking conceals your phone number each time you place a call, without having to enter a code each time. Whenever you use either of these services, the Caller I.D. box of the person you're calling will say something like "private," "unavailable," or "anonymous."

In addition to blocking your own caller I.D., you can also refuse the calls of those who block. Anonymous Call Rejection is a service that rejects all calls from people who block. If you use this service, your phone won't even ring; the person calling you will be treated to a recorded message saying you don't accept blocked calls.

This can get out of hand. Let's say you have Caller I.D. and you're really into it. Man, do you love your Caller I.D. You just *love* finding out who's on the phone before you answer, and you hate it when you can't get that information. You hate it so much you don't even want to *receive* those calls, so you have your phone refuse calls from those who block, you hypocrite. Now pretend that your friend Wendy feels the same way. You both have Anonymous Call Rejection. That means neither of your phones will accept calls from those who block identifying information, and you have both chosen to do exactly that. Now you and Wendy can no longer talk on the phone from home because your phone blocks her calls and vice versa. The only way you can reach each other is to call from a different phone number or have an operator assist you in placing the call. This just can't be what Alexander Graham Bell had in mind.

CALL RETURN

Call Return, which is frequently referred to as *69, is a service that most residential customers can access. It allows your phone to dial back the phone that called you most recently, simply by pressing—exactly!—*69.

As with Caller I.D., the very existence of this service has probably reduced the number of mischievous pubescents out there crowded around a telephone and ordering fifteen anchovy pizzas delivered to their math teacher's address. And Call Return can indeed be a handy function. If Jeff called you from his sister's apartment for directions to your house, and you didn't realize until you hung up that when you said "left" you meant "right," what could you do if you had no idea what his sister's phone number was? You could dial *69. How handy!

In many cases, its use is less friendly and the rules are murkier. What about when you answer the phone and for the third time that day the person hangs up? You could call back, but what would you say? "Hey, quit it." Maybe. It's worth thinking it through before you try.

There are also times when Call Return won't work. If you try to use Call Return to reach someone who blocks identifying information, you will hear a recorded announcement explaining that the number cannot be reached by that service.

CONFERENCE CALLS

Conference calling allows three or more parties to participate in a conversation on a single phone line simultaneously—today's version of a party line. For a small conference call, you would establish a call with one of the parties, push down the switch hook, and dial the second party. When you pushed down the switch hook again, everyone would be connected and the conference could begin.

On a call involving lots of people, the phone company or a private company usually gets involved to link the calls through a central computer. Sometimes large conference calls are coordinated by an operator, and some have a single phone number, often toll-free, that participants dial to take part.

As with other services, it is very important to make sure you know how to work the technology before you initiate a conference call. No one likes getting put on hold indefinitely or getting cut off or told "No, just a sec. I think I—no, wait—" and, believe it or not, it's not a terribly impressive thing to do. Practice at least once on patient friends or coworkers before you try to use the conference call function in an important meeting.

The cardinal rule for conference calls is that expected participants must be informed in advance of the exact time of the call. All involved parties must clear their calendars, hold their other calls, and have relevant information at the ready. It is very impolite to spring a conference call on someone who is not expecting it. Likewise, it is terribly rude to make others wait while you gather and shuffle the papers you will need to refer to.

Of course, business folk know they sometimes will be hit with something they didn't plan for. But let's say you and Emily are talking about the big deal and you realize that John should really be in on the call. Instead of calling him into the conference call directly, either you or Emily should call him on another line to ask if he can take part.

Once you're up and gabbing, make a great effort to wait until someone is done speaking before you add your brilliant two cents. It's hard not to interrupt people in a conference call. The visual cues that you get in a face-to-face meeting aren't there to stop you. People tend to cut in and overlap their dialogue, but it's unprofessional, so don't do it.

Screening Calls

It's basically a given that you don't want to talk to everyone who calls you when they call. You're a busy person with important things to do!

In a time not that long ago, you could leave your phone off the hook or let it continue to ring if you were not in the mood to talk. You know what? You can still employ those time-tested strategies. But now that technology has given you some new choices, such as answering machines and Caller I.D., there's a whole new set of possibilities.

You can allow your answering machine to pick up the call, listen to find out who is leaving the message, and decide whether or not to pick up the call. If you don't pick up the call, and the caller is not calling from a cellular phone outside your window where he can see you sneaking around, he'll never know you were screening, and that's good. If you do pick up, he'll know you were screening, but he'll be pleased that you deem him worthy of your telephone time. There's just one problem: You'll get a reputation as a screener. Before long your friends will leave messages like this: "Are you screening your calls? Pick up. I have to talk to you. Come on. I know you're there," and that will probably annoy you a lot. Even when you aren't home, people who know you as a screener will wonder why you're not taking their calls. Of course, it's your prerogative. No one says you have to talk to someone on the phone at a particular time just because that's when they feel like talking to you. Heavens, no. But people's feelings do get hurt.

With Caller I.D. you don't have to wait for the machine to pick up to find out who is calling. You can decide whether or not to speak to a person while the phone is still ringing, with a quick glance at the Caller I.D. screen. Sure, it's an invasion of privacy, but the telephone is by nature an instrument of intrusion, so tough noogies. There's an additional benefit to screening your calls, especially with Caller I.D.: Say your fifteen-year-old son's best friend is calling and you hate talking to him because he's a boring mumbler—if you know it's him calling before you pick up the phone, you can have your son answer the phone, or just let it ring if your son's not home.

Screening calls is, of course, not a practice confined to the home. In offices in which people do not answer their own phones, receptionists and assistants have long been human screeners. It's a delicate job. It is the responsibility of the person for whom the calls are being screened to give the assistant a list of people who should be put through no matter what—and those who shouldn't. The most important thing for the person answering the phones to remember is to put the caller on hold so she doesn't hear the person she's trying to reach say, "That boring freak! No way. Tell her I'm out with malaria."

Different Rules for Different Phones

You didn't think this was going to be simple, did you? There are so many different technologies out there, which means there are also different things you can get away with. Sure, you can pick your nose while you're talking on a speaker phone, but maybe you shouldn't when at a public phone, and certainly not on a video phone. Equipment sometimes dictates the rules and you need to be mindful of the various characteristics of different technologies, and the right and wrong ways to use them.

SPEAKER PHONES

In addition to the traditional handset, speaker phones generally also have a microphone and speaker built in to the base to amplify the sound.

There are not too many people out there who like to be spoken to by someone using his speaker phone. The implication seems to be that he is very busy doing something other than talking on the phone. It is extremely impolite to use the speaker-phone function without first asking the permission of the person to whom you are speaking. It is not at all impolite to ask someone to take you off speaker phone. If the person complains, he is doubly rude, and you should tell on him.

Unfortunately, there is one exception to this rule. If there weren't, perhaps we could dump speaker-phone technology once and for all. But there are times when a group of people at one location need to speak with another, or group of others, at a different location. Sure, the snazzier ones out there may use video conferencing, but not everyone has the capability. There is one important rule for such group speaker-phone situations: It is required that all the people in the room be identified to the person or people on the other end of the line.

Let's say Paul and Ringo are on a speaker phone, having a conversation with George. And let's say George only hears Paul's voice and doesn't know Ringo's in the room. There's nothing to stop him from slipping in a jab about the vocals on "Octopus's Garden." Sure, it's not that nice to do it behind Ringo's back, but imagine how much worse George will feel about saying it directly to his speaker-phone face. Paul should tell George that Ringo is there. (But somehow, of course, Yoko will get blamed for the whole mess.)

PAY PHONES

Ideally, when calling from a public pay phone, you should use a credit or calling card, so your call will not be interrupted by disconnection threats. Of course, this is not always possible. If you do find yourself using coins for a pay-phone conversation, you should inform the person you're calling of your situation right after you greet him. If you realize you are running out of coins, it is acceptable to ask the other person to call you back if you have a preexisting relationship with him. In other words, if you're calling about a potential job, don't ask for a call back to a phone booth. But if you're talking to your bowling buddy, Frankie, go for it. If you are going to ask someone to return your call at a public phone, be sure to do so before the cycle of recorded messages begins— because they can be extraordinarily disruptive to the conversation and annoying to the participants.

If there are people waiting for the phone, however, finish your call and move along; it is not fair for them to have to wait for someone to call you back. Likewise, if you expect to make more than one phone call and there is someone—or a group of people— waiting for the phone, at the very least inform them of your situation. If you're going to be calling a dozen people and only one person is waiting, it would be really nice to let him go ahead of you, don't you think?

It has lately become important that you determine the local or long-distance carrier on the phones you use. Some charge more than three times as much as others. Knowing how to access your preferred carrier can save you lots of money.

Except in the case of prior arrangement or, of course, in case of an emergency, you should never call someone else collect. This rule is null and void if you are (a) calling your spouse or equivalent, (b) in college and calling your parents, or (c) trying to end a relationship with the person you are calling.

VIDEO PHONES

Video phones are still used most commonly in the cartoon world of the future. They can be hooked up either through a computer or a separate system that uses a TV screen. Video-phone cameras take frequent pictures and transmit them via modem.

Video phones are still cost-prohibitive for the masses. Even those who can afford to buy them are frequently unwilling to, basically because their friends won't be able to play with them; it would be like having one walkie-talkie. Further, there are still complaints about the technology's slow, jerky, grainy picture. The picture quality has improved over the years, but it cannot yet support enough frames per second to provide the TV quality we expect.

If you should find yourself engaged in a video call or conference, use your common sense. Act as you would in person, but be mindful of which parts of your body are included in the camera's range and which are not. If hand gestures are crucial to the point you wish to make, consider your camera angle before you start talking, because a *Can you see what I'm doing here?* kind of conversation isn't much fun for anyone.

Special Rules for Home Businesses

Home businesses have been on the rise for years. That means it's not quite as surprising when you call a company expecting a receptionist, and instead get a four-year-old. One of the best investments a home business can make is the installation of a separate phone line. When the business line rings, you know how to answer it. If only the kids are home, they know *not* to answer it. Many clients and would-be clients expect professionalism. And while you may be the very best at what you do, a teenager answering your phone with "Yo?" will not create a favorable impression.

Since most of your customers will never get to see the office with which they do business—whether it's a desk in the corner of your den, a separate room in your home, or a workstation in the pantry—let them envision what we used to think of as a "real office." One simple way to achieve that is to treat the phone as professionals do. If you use a machine or call-answering service, make sure your message sounds professional (i.e., no garbage truck noise from the street or television sounds in the background).

If you work out of your home and have a single phone line, Call Answering is mandatory. A client who is trying to reach you must be able to leave a message for you whether you are unable to answer the phone or on another call. Call Waiting is not a viable alternative. In promoting an appearance of professionalism, it is very important that your clients believe they have your undivided attention; Call Waiting accomplishes the exact opposite.

You should also be sure to become acquainted with special services your phone company may offer for home businesses. Some offer a variety of telephone rings on a single telephone to indicate calls to different numbers (as in one long ring—*brrriiiiinng*—to signify a call to your home's personal line, and two quick rings—*bringbring*—to signify a call for your office).

It is important, too, to routinely reexamine the way in which you use your phone. If you realize that you spend a good portion of the workday online and you have only one phone line, ask yourself how your customers are ever going to reach you by telephone. Even though the initial expense may seem like a less fun way to spend the money than, say, on a giant tub of M&Ms, a dedicated business phone line is pretty much indispensable for a growing home business.

chapter two

Cellular
telephones

TECHNO—FACTS:
how cellular phones work

Cellular phones, as you no doubt know, are wireless phones that you can use almost anywhere (though of course if you're a polite and savvy techno-user, you know that you shouldn't). Cell phones have built-in radio transmitters and receivers. A **transmitter** is a device that sends an electrical signal through the air. A **receiver** is a device that receives these electrical signals. (Picture this: Radio stations have transmitters and your radio is a receiver.)

When you make a call from your cellular phone, it transmits radio signals to a **cell station**. The cell station, which services a particular geographic area or cell, then alerts the **mobile telephone switching office** (**MTSO**). The MTSO connects your call to your good old regular local phone company, which puts the call through to the number you're dialing, be it a regular phone or another cellular phone.

Another way to think about it is that each cell station has a radius (envision a circle). These circles overlap so that as your phone transmits a message, the signal goes out to your cell station, and all overlapping stations. When you cross a barrier to another cell, the other cell will pick you up.

Like regular phones, cellular phones can be either digital or analog, and many cellular service providers offer the same phone services as your local phone company, such as Call Waiting, conference calling, and voice mail.

Cellular Phone Etiquette

Cellular phones have become so affordable that they are no longer a reliable indicator of a major Hollywood player. Now that person with the technology pressed up to his ear is just as likely to be a real estate agent or a high school kid. One of the problems is that many people still *feel* like big shots when they use cellular phones, and what's more irritating, they act like big shots.

The great irony of cellular phone etiquette, of course, is that the people who most need it—the biggest big shots—are the least likely to care. But there's a horde of us who sometimes need to use our cellular phones and don't want to be misconstrued as big shot wanna-bes. Have no fear; just follow these simple rules and call from your cell phone in the morning.

INSTRUMENT OF LAST RESORT

Cellular phones have begun to permeate the modern landscape. Once upon a time, people had to seek out a public phone to make a call. There were not telephones available wherever you went. One of the lovely by-products of this was that there wasn't someone *talking on the phone* wherever you went. Now there is. Back then, people had to go to private areas, known by the quaint term *phone booths*, to make their calls. No one but the person to whom they were talking could hear them. Now people can call from wherever they want, and they do, and we can hear them. It doesn't mean it's right. Phone calls were meant to be private.

Those who use their cell phones frequently insist they are necessary. Sometimes they are. But usually they're not. Use your cell phone in public only when no other means of communication is viable, and even then, only when it will not pose an annoyance threat to those around you, even if those around you are strangers you'll never see again.

When you are out socially, you should not use your cell phone except in a discreet, private way. At a table in a nightclub with your date and another couple is neither discreet nor private. The people with whom you are dining deserve your undivided attention for as long as you're sitting together. So what do you do if your friend does this to you, with a quick call to the baby-sitter or to check his voice mail? You could look shocked, express your outrage, and/or force him to explain. But no explanation is going to be a good one. The trouble with cellular-phone rudeness is that the guilty party doesn't see the problem. Chances are if you tell him you're offended, he'll find a way to take offense himself, the big jerk. All you can do is prevent it from happening again by inviting different people to join you at the nightclub next time.

What about the loudmouth on the cellular phone at the table next to you in a restaurant? Your subtle dirty looks probably won't work. If you carry this book around with you, you may want to highlight this section and delicately place it between his bread plate and water glass. If you feel comfortable, you can politely ask if he would mind keeping it down. To avoid a direct confrontation, you can ask a grown-up—in this case, a member of the wait-staff—to handle the situation—after all, this person is ruining your dining experience. The waiter or waitress may ask if you would like to be moved to a different table. It's not ideal to have to pick up your drinks and move—the cell-phone guy is the one breaking social rules—but if it makes your meal more enjoyable, just do it.

Don't forget that talking on the phone does require some concentration, which means some attention will be diverted from whatever else you might be doing at the same time. When you are crossing a busy street, you should not be talking on a cellular phone.

You should also be aware that there are places where you should never ever use your cellular phone: a house of worship (it will guarantee you a ride on the express to hell); any drive-through, such as a bank or fast-food restaurant; certain areas within hospitals and medical offices, and at designated times on airplanes, as the phone can interfere with radio-based monitoring equipment;

and any auditorium-like room with people who paid to be there (concert) or people who would pay not to be there (school play).

Also: in the driver's seat. But we'll get to that in a minute.

ON THE RECEIVING END

Turn your cellular phone off—except in private or emergency situations. If you have a cellular phone, chances are you can afford a beeper. When in social situations, direct calls to your beeper, and keep it on vibration mode. This goes for business as well as social situations—meetings, movies, conferences, restaurants. People did not go out to an evening of fine dining only to listen to you close a huge deal.

While there may be slightly greater leeway in business than in social situations, it is always inconsiderate to have your cellular phone on and ringing while you are in the company of other people. If you absolutely must keep your cell phone on during a meeting, you should apologize in advance for the inconvenience. People have every right to roll their eyes at you; the people with whom you are meeting deserve your undivided attention.

It *always* bears reexamination: Are you doing it because you have to or because you can? Before you decide to go ahead and be kind of rude and accept a phone call at a meeting or in any situation at which others are present, make sure you have no other viable alternatives. Could someone else at your office accept the call for you? Could you direct the phone call to a beeper, excuse yourself from the meeting with apologies, and call the person back? Is there a voice-mail box that you could direct the call to?

Are you just being a big, fat show-off or is this call truly unavoidable?

HOW TO TALK ON A CELLULAR PHONE IN PUBLIC

QUIETLY. Talk loud enough that the person to whom you are speaking can hear you, and no louder. Be respectful of the people around you. If you're in a small, crowded area, is it really necessary that you call at that time? Can you get to a more private location before placing your call? Most people would rather *not* overhear your conversation, fascinating as it may be.

BE PREPARED, LITTLE SCOUT

The reason you have a cellular phone in the first place is to be able to stay in touch when you're not near a regular telephone. So what happens when your cell-phone battery loses its charge? You're back in the same position. If your cellular phone matters to you that much and you expect to use it a lot, you should be mindful of the level of the battery's charge and you should also carry a spare, charged battery. Even if you're diligent about recharging your battery between uses, you should remember that at some point even rechargeable batteries can just wear out. (If your charged battery doesn't last nearly as long as it used to, it's time to think about replacing it.) If you are cellular-reliant, keep a spare battery everywhere—with the phone, in the car, in your briefcase.

And remember that in those B.C. years—before cellular—people were still able to do business. Have a credit or calling card with you and use one of those charming phone booths. If you don't

have a credit or calling card, keep loose change—especially quarters—available.

JUST BECAUSE EVERYONE DOES IT DOESN'T MEAN IT'S RIGHT

Using technology impolitely can be a problem. But using it in
ways it shouldn't be used is also extremely dangerous, as anyone
who watches the news knows. Too many accidents happen when
drivers are talking on cellular phones. How important can all these
calls be that people endanger not just their lives, but yours, too?

When is it okay to call from your car? When it's parked or when
someone else is driving. It's true; you see people putting on
makeup or shaving while talking on the phone and driving their
cars down busy highways. You also often see major accidents on
the side of the road. Coincidence? I think not. The statistics are
very disturbing: The number of accidents that occur while the
driver is talking on the phone is as high as the number of accidents
that occur while the driver is under the influence of alcohol. People who have caused an accident because they were talking on or
answering a cellular phone have been clobbered in lawsuits. So
why do it?

Driving safely requires your complete attention. Except for on
certain stretches of the Pacific Coast Highway, it's usually very
easy to pull off a road to have a conversation. And that's what you
should do. Really. In the rare, emergency instances during which
you must speak while driving, at least keep the following tips in
mind.

Always let the person to whom you are speaking know that you are calling from a car, and perhaps she won't mind if you put her on the speaker phone, with her permission. Speaker phones are rude; you heard it here. But when you're driving, it's safety first, courtesy second. Another benefit to informing your caller about your mobile situation is that she is likely to help keep the conversation shorter. She's heard the frightening statistics about talking on the phone while driving and doesn't want any part in the accident you're cruising toward.

You may be tempted to buy an earphone/headset/microphone adapter for your cellular phone to use in place of the speaker phone. This is fine if you plan to pull over and use it. But when you're driving, you need to be able to hear what is going on around you, and earphones cut you off from important noises (like honking horns and screeching brakes) that could alert you to a potentially dangerous situation.

You'll be safer if you keep your cellular phone off while you're traveling. The bad people who might pirate or clone your phone number and use it for their own calls can't do so when your phone is off, so there's an added bonus in decreasing your chances of being ripped off. This is also important in terms of driving safety: What if the phone's ring jars you and you jump in your seat at a critical driving time? At the very least, turn the volume down on the ringer so that it doesn't catch you off guard. When the phone rings, get to a place where you can safely pull over before answering. If you must pick up a call while you're driving, don't answer the phone near busy intersections or difficult stretches of road. People are accustomed to waiting for a few rings before a cell-phone call is answered, and even if they're not, they'll get over it. If you answer while driving, ask the caller to please hold until you can pull over and continue the conversation.

There are cellular phones that allow you to send faxes and even e-mail, but of course you would never consider using this technology while you're driving. Because you're a responsible person who knows that a parking lot is the right place to telecommunicate.

Perhaps the best advice is to use your phone for good, not evil. To reiterate: Unless it's urgent, don't talk on the phone and drive; it's not necessary and is an unsafe and irresponsible thing to do. On the other hand, when you see people in dangerous situations— accidents on the side of the road or hazardous conditions on a roadway, for example—get to a safe place and call for help.

PRIVACY AND SECURITY

Even if you're all by your lonesome in a padded cell, you should always remember the limited privacy a cellular phone affords you. If you read the papers or watch the news, you know that cellular calls are not secure. That should lead you to realize that you shouldn't discuss anything over a cellular phone that you would like to remain confidential. Especially if you're a politician. Don't forget: You conducted business before the cellular phone was invented and placed in your hands. You can still communicate in other ways, particularly when it involves information that needs to be kept confidential. If a face-to-face conversation is not possible, try using the U.S. Postal Service.

There is one other important thing you can do to protect yourself in this mean world. Most cellular services provide personal identification numbers (PINs) to prevent thieves who steal phones from using them with ease. Don't deactivate your PIN and don't make it easy for the bad guys by programming your PIN into a speed-dial function.

chapter three

was that

Yours or Mine?

TECHNO-FACTS:

how beepers work

When you call a beeper (also known as a pager), you're not actually dialing directly into that little box clipped to the belt loop of the person you're trying to reach. You are using your telephone to dial into a whole **paging terminal**. Here's how it works. That tone you hear after you dial the beeper number is the paging terminal's way of indicating that it's time to enter your message (which, for a numeric pager, you do by entering the phone number at which you want to be called back and then, on most models, pressing the pound (#) key and hanging up). The paging terminal, which is linked to transmitters, converts your message into a code which it then sends out as a radio signal throughout its area or range. The pager with the matching code—the one you're calling—will then display the message and respond appropriately by beeping, vibrating, or whistling "Dixie."

Modern pagers can do a lot more than beep or give your leg a thrill. While the notification—a beep or vibration—is the same as it ever was, now, instead of showing a phone number, alphanumeric pagers can display a typed message. While these handy gadgets can often eliminate the need to return the call— certain models can handle really long messages—some may require more technology than a phone on the callers' end. To leave an alphanumeric message, you must use a modem or special device designed precisely for this purpose, or speak to an operator who will enter your message for you. There are also beepers that actually record and replay callers' voice messages. Some can even receive e-mail.

But beepers have their drawbacks. With many, if you're paged and you're out of range, you'll simply never receive the message, but some models store messages that are received while you're out of range and deliver them as soon as you return.

BEEPER ETIQUETTE

Beeper etiquette is simple. There is one clear and steadfast rule: Except in the privacy of your own home, your beeper should never be on beep mode. It should always be on vibration mode.

Why would anyone ever need it to beep? All that does is disrupt and annoy other people. Say you're in a meeting you don't want to be in. You wore your beeper because you told your friend Danny to beep you in a half hour so you could excuse yourself. If you have really sunken to this level of desperation, you can achieve the same goal with vibration mode. Pull at your beeper in an exaggerated fashion. Squint at the screen that displays the number. Mime some lame apology and leave the room. (Danny doesn't even need to bother calling for you to put on this charade.)

There's no excuse. If you're going to the social event of the century and wearing a clingy, slinky number to which you cannot attach a beeper, you shouldn't bring it at all. No one at the big gala wants to hear your beeper. No one *ever* wants to hear your beeper. Beeping mode should not exist. In fact, the only reason it does exist is so that we don't have to call them vibrators.

chapter four

the many talents of your

Phone Line

TECHNO—FACTS:
how modems and ISDNs work

Your phone line can do ever so much more than reach out and touch someone with a phone call. A phone line can provide the means for computers to talk directly to each other or through a network, and for fax machines to transmit to each other or to computers.

A **modem** is a device that enables your computer to talk to other computers over traditional analog phone lines. Its name derived from its function—MOdulate/DEModulate. A modem takes a computer's digital information and translates (modulates) it into analog waves that can be transmitted over plain old telephone service (POTS) lines. Then the modem at the receiving end reverses the process (demodulates).

When discussing their modems, people will frequently refer

to their baud rates. A **baud rate** is how fast information gets sent over an analog line and is measured in bits per second. For example, a 28.8 modem transmits 28,800 bits per second. (Be forewarned: For real computer nerds, this can lead to "my pop is bigger than your pop" discussions.) **Bandwidth** is a more general term that describes a medium's capacity for carrying information, or the amount of data that can be transmitted over a medium in a given amount of time.

Bear in mind that what you read today could be laughably outdated by next month, but at this writing, most computer connections are by phone line, for obvious reasons. People already *have* phone lines in their offices and homes, and connecting by modem is a relatively simple process. But other possibilities do exist, and you should know what they are so you can nod knowledgeably when people talk about them.

ISDN (it stands for **Integrated Services Digital Network**) is a system of digital phone connections that allows data to be transmitted over POTS lines in a completely digital form. The only difference between an analog phone line and an ISDN phone line is the system to which the line is connected at your local phone company.

You may also hear people talk about transferring data over a traditional television cable using a **cable modem**. Traditionally, the cable system was a series of copper wires called coaxial or coax (pronounced co-ax) that connected homes to the cable company. These days cable companies are replacing the old copper wires with newer, high-speed fiber-optic cables that can carry more information with less interference and transmit it faster in digital format. Many cable systems today use a combination of the two, called hybrid fiber coax (HFC), in which fiber-optic lines carry data from the cable company to your street, and copper lines carry the data from the street to your house. Just like an ISDN, the cable system allows people to transmit/receive completely digital signals.

There is also a way to connect your home computer to the outside world without any cables or phone lines—a satellite dish can send your data in digital form with no nasty wires to trip over!

(Nothing But the) Fax

TECHNO—FACTS:
how fax machines work

Even the most techno-phobic among us have probably had occasion to use a fax machine. They have vastly sped up the business of correspondence. What used to be packed up into an overnight envelope is now placed on the fax machine and instantly transmitted to another fax machine (or computer) through the phone lines.

A fax machine scans an image by reading it digitally, and then, because telephone lines right now are mostly analog, translates it into an analog signal, and transmits it over the phone lines, to be converted back into a digital signal and read on the receiving end.

Because all fax machines operate differently, the opportunities for making a fool of yourself still exist. At the top of the list is placing the papers up when they should be down, or vice versa. Picture, if you will, your fifteen-page report printing out as blank sheets on your newest client's fax machine. This is worth avoiding. If you share a machine in an office, you might just casually note how someone else loads their outgoing papers, or be radical and actually ask for help. If it's your own machine, read the guide. (And if you've tried to send a fax from your office four times and it still won't go through, and you work in one of those offices in which you have to dial nine to access an outside phone line, well, you do the math.)

NEATNESS COUNTS!

While fax machines provide a slightly more casual way to communicate quickly, business rules still apply. In a formal business environment, think of a fax machine as a superefficient envelope; don't send anything you wouldn't mail. In other words, just because it's a fax doesn't mean it can be sloppy, dog-eared, and scratched-out. Keep your copy clean. Make sure the text is dark— preferably black or red, as blue does not transmit well. If you are adding handwritten notes to the document, use a dark pen and write clearly. As always, different rules apply if you're just messing around with your friends. If you're sending a copy of the engagement notice of your high school girlfriend to your best friend, coffee stains and editorial comments are acceptable.

As with all technologies, it helps to keep in mind some of the problems you've encountered on the receiving end. Think about the difficulties you've had with faxes you've gotten. If appropriate, use an easy-to-read font in a large point size to ensure easy readability. Try to work with larger margins, especially at the bottom and top of your pages; fax machines are notorious for cutting off copy. And when it can be avoided, don't fax a document that was faxed to you, or your faxee may receive slanted, unreadable copy.

COVER ME

Cover sheets are usually a good idea. There are also little Post-it forms that you can place directly on the document, which provide you with a space to write all the relevant information. The most important information to include is your name, phone number, fax number, number of pages being faxed (being clear about whether the number includes the cover sheet), and the date the fax was sent. Again, always think about the recipient. If you're sending a fax to your friend Bill, whose fax machine sits next to his coffee-maker in his studio apartment, and you, Bill's partner, and Bill's mother are the only ones who send him faxes, Bill can probably figure out who sent the fax even if you don't use a cover sheet. (Unless Bill's dumb.) But if you're sending a fax to Bill at the office, be sure to include his last name and yours, and to keep the cover sheet free of private information.

CALL AHEAD?

What about the notorious call to the intended recipient of the fax before it is transmitted? Some think it's required; others find it an intolerable nuisance. If you think about the situation of the recipient, the need/advisability of a call-ahead should be obvious. For example, some people have fax/modems in their computers. These folks would naturally need to be advised to turn their computers on and set up the appropriate program. Many home businesses have fax machines that share a phone line with regular telephone service. These people need to set up their machines by turning a switch in the phone line and would thus require a call-ahead. If you are on the receiving end of a fax, it is your responsibility to let the sender know if you will require a call-ahead.

If you're sending a fax to a fairly large company, or someone whom you know has a dedicated phone line connected to a fax machine, a cover sheet should accomplish most of what you would achieve with a call-ahead. As with any good rule, however, there are exceptions to this one. If you want to be sure the fax gets to the desk of the recipient quickly, a call-ahead to confirm the fax number or to confirm that the recipient is in can do the trick. (This can also be accomplished with a post-fax wrap-up call, e.g., "Just wanted to let Dr. Hughes know I sent the fax.") Before you place a call-ahead, make sure your document is ready to go and the fax machine is not in use, being serviced, or broken. Your call should be followed by your fax within fifteen minutes (not hours or days).

Here's some potentially life- (or at least job-) saving information: The most important call-ahead, the one you must always remember—the mother of all call-aheads—is the call-ahead for personal-information-sent-to-a-workplace fax. When you want to fax your buddy a copy of your newborn's tush, you should know that a call-ahead is in order.

WHEN NOT TO FAX

There are times when you should never fax. Newsflash: When companies request that you not fax your résumé, they're not joking. Most offices that make this request simply do not want to have their machines tied up all day with a deluge of résumés (or menus, for that matter). Many will toss faxed résumés in the trash; some particularly vindictive human resources professionals have been known to wait until the mail arrives and toss out the résumés mailed in from those who also disobeyed the no-fax ordinance.

When you have a very long document to send someone—more than a dozen pages—pause to reconsider. No one likes a clogged-up fax machine. People in your office will be forced to wait for your transmission to go through, as will those on the receiving end. If there is another viable way to get your document to its intended recipient, such as by overnight mail, do it. Remember, just because a super-speedy technology is available doesn't mean you have to use it.

It may be tempting to send a fax when the thought of a face-to-face encounter is too difficult to consider. People have resigned and been fired by fax. This can only be described as very bad form. When you're ready to let that no-good Jones go, you can't just fax him a short message informing him that as of week's end, he's history, toast, kaput. This is not the way the big boys and girls play. It happens, but it's not right.

Speaking of wrong things to do, confidential information should not be sent by fax. While you may assume that faxes are treated in much the same way as United States Post Office letters (also known as snail mail), in many cases, they're not. As people deliver faxes to the person to whom they have been sent, they sometimes cannot keep their eyes from scanning the page; faxed documents are the techno-equivalent of the picture postcard. And it's not uncommon to send a fax to the wrong number. It is wise, therefore, to discuss confidential material in person, or on a telephone (not cellular), or to send it by snail mail. But, of course, not on a picture postcard.

You should also consider the implications of the fax machine. Imagine that you represent one of nine companies competing for a new client's project, and your proposal is the only one that's faxed. The other eight arrived in the mail or by overnight carrier. You may give the impression of being a last-minute operator. Not only that, the other eight proposals were probably submitted on creamy, heavy stock papers. Yours is on shiny, annoyingly curled fax paper. Good luck.

Online and Upward

oversimplified intro to Computers

TECHNO-FACTS:
how computers work

There are many nearly competent computer users out there tiptoeing their way through computer conversations, hoping that the topic doesn't veer from the *exact things* they understand. *Don't ask me about cache!* they may silently chant as the conversation turns in that direction, or *For crying out loud, please don't let this get into CPUs.* Worse still, they do not fully understand their machines and cannot perform any tasks or functions beyond the six they use every day.

While you may not need to know how a computer works in order to get out on the Internet and learn what time the new buddy-cop movie is showing at your neighborhood theater, you may still find it helpful. The more you know about the way things work, the better your chances for using them with a modicum of professionalism and courtesy. Here, at its most basic, is a guide to understanding computers.

When you see a computer with a screen, a separate keyboard, mouse, and computer system (the stuff in the big plastic or metal box, which some people inaccurately call the CPU), you are looking at a desktop or **personal computer (PC)**.

Most popular PCs today are based on the WINTEL paradigm, which means they use the Intel Central Processing Unit and the Microsoft Windows operating system. The original PC was introduced by IBM in the early 1980s and the WINTEL PCs—IBMs and IBM clones—are based on this model. Useful tip for beginners: Macintosh computers, even when they look just like the desktop computers described above, are not called PCs. They are always Macs. Go figure.

The small computer that people carry with them, which has a self-contained computer system and opens to display a built-in keyboard, mouse, and screen, is a **laptop**. (Just to complicate the landscape, portable Macintosh computers *can* be called laptops, and are also known as Powerbooks.) A **sub-notebook** is a very small laptop. **Personal digital assistants (PDAs)** are computers that can be held in your hand and are most often used for simple daily tasks, like storing contact information and to-do lists, though they can handle more intensive computer functions, too.

Now, just for kicks, let's try to understand, in oversimplified terms, how a computer works. The **central processing unit (CPU)** is the heart of the computer, where all the instructions are executed. **RAM (random access memory)**, is the memory area where programs and your data must be in order to do stuff. The **hard disk**, which is also called the **hard drive**, is where you store information. Look at it this way: In order for the CPU to do the actual business of computers (work on a word-processing document, run a spreadsheet, etc.), it has to load the data and/or program into something called memory; the CPU can't work on data when it's on the hard drive—it has to be in memory. The CPU has to issue instructions to load the data or program that's stored on the hard disk into RAM so that it can process it. But the funny thing about RAM (really, it's so funny) is that when you turn your computer off, it's gone. Have you ever lost power while you were editing a document in memory? Did you lose your file? You may have wondered where it went. If you did not save it back to the hard disk, it disappeared with the ephemeral RAM. This is important: What's on the hard disk is saved when you turn off the computer, but what is in RAM is not.

This thing we've been calling RAM is made up of chips. If you'd like, you may picture them as potato chips but, in fact, they are somewhat smaller and much less tasty. Some RAM chips are faster than others. The fastest of all is known as **cache** (pronounced the same as *cash*). These chips speed things up by swiftly moving data between RAM and the CPU.

Obviously, the programs and data on your computer have to be stored somewhere. The hard disk, as we have noted, is where you store most of the stuff you use on your computer. (That groaning, whizzing sound you sometimes hear your computer making is the hard drive at work. Good to know it's not loafing, eh?) A **floppy disk**, which is not terribly floppy, is, like a hard disk, a storage device, but one that has much less space and that is portable—it goes in the disk drive with a gentle shove and comes out at the push of a button. (In the old days, by the way, they *were* floppy.) A **floppy disk drive** is that opening into which you insert your floppy disk (only one at a time, by the way) and is responsible for transferring the data on your floppy disk to the computer's memory.

Here's a fact to live by: You should always back up every single file that you'd be annoyed to lose. **Backing up** is making a copy of a computer document. Most people back up their stuff to floppy disk. You should keep backup disks separate from your computer. If someone steals all your computer stuff, you want your disks far from the scene of the crime so they're spared. Or if a fire should claim your computer, a nearby shelf of backup disks would also be reduced to ash. Storing work stuff at home and vice versa is a safe bet, as is a bank's safe deposit box.

If you have a great deal of data to back up, you have some options. As fate would have it, the fastest ones are the most expensive and the slowest are the most affordable. Your hard disk tops the list; it's fast, but by comparison, buying a new one costs righteous bucks. You can also invest in a Zip drive or its cheaper cousin, a tape drive. Both are storage devices that hold much more information than a floppy disk.

While hard disks and floppy disks are used primarily for storing data, there's another medium from which you can *read* information. It's the compact disc (CD), which is read by your **CD-ROM (compact disc read-only memory)**. "Read only" means you can't save your data on a compact disc; you use CDs (which look just like the music kind) to access information that is already stored on them (like an encyclopedia or a game). Because light is used to record data on a CD, as opposed to the magnetic heads on a disk, CDs can store about five hundred times the data that can be stored on a floppy disk.

Digital versatile disks (DVDs), like CD-ROMs, are used for computer data storage, but are designed specifically to store video and audio; one disk can store a full-length movie. (These are currently being touted as the cutting-edge replacement for those dusty old VHS tapes, audio cassette tapes, and even CDs of yesteryear.)

OTHER NIFTY COMPUTER TERMS TO BANDY ABOUT

Computer **hardware** is the physical components that make up your computer. (You can see and touch it.)

Software is the programs that allow you to interact with your computer and that make your computer work.

A computer **virus** is a malicious program intended to corrupt your software.

A **scanner,** like a fax machine, reads through an image by scanning it line by line. It translates this information into a digital format which can be stored on the hard disk and read by programs that show it on your screen, many in full color.

A **printer** receives instructions from your computer that enable it to produce a printed version of your document. A wide variety of printers are available—from the old dot-matrix models to color laser printers.

Hard copy is a printed-out version of a computer document.

A **modem** is a device that translates digital information from a computer to analog data that can be sent over a phone line and vice versa.

Logging on establishes a connection to another computer.

Logging off terminates your connection to another computer.

You are **online** when your computer is hooked up to another, usually by a modem connection.

You go **offline** when you terminate your computer's connection to another, even if you're still working on your computer.

MODEM OR FAX/MODEM?

Most modems today also function as fax machines (and are called **fax/modems**). What's the difference? Glad you asked. If someone faxes a document to your computer, you will receive a document that you can read—a simple screen or printed image. But unless you have special character-recognition software, you cannot edit it or manipulate it on your computer; you can only read it. (If you do have character-recognition software, it can translate the image into a form that can be understood by word-processing software.)

Now, if someone sends a document to you by modem, and both computers have the same software (let's say the same word-processing program), you will receive a computer document that you *can* work on. It will be as though you were sent a floppy disk containing the document.

chapter six

E-mail basics

You don't need to be up and running on the Internet to send e-mail (electronic mail). Many companies without online capabilities have e-mail programs in their computer network systems. An **e-mail program** is just what you think it is—a program that allows you to type a message on your computer and, with the click of a mouse, send it to someone else who also has e-mail capabilities. Of course it also allows you to receive messages.

Many e-mail systems can still only accommodate **ASCII (American Standard Code for Information Interchange)** text, which means that messages don't include graphics or even basic formatting (bold, center, italic). The fact that you are limited to ASCII text means you can pretty much use only those type functions that are available on a standard typewriter. You can use the letters A through Z, the numbers 0 through 9, punctuation, and a handful of miscellaneous keys (#%&). Even if your mail system allows you to send more complex documents like graphics, the person on the other end may not be able to receive them.

Typing a message using ASCII text is not vastly different from typing a letter to a friend. But *sending* your e-mail message is a whole different ball o' wax. Let's take a look at an e-mail address: sassyone@dragnet.org. The **user name** (sassyone) appears before the @ sign. It is usually of the person's own choosing, and will often be his first and/or last name or some combination thereof. The **domain name** (dragnet) appears after the @ sign and is the name of the computer or network of computers where the address is located. After the domain name there is an even higher designation—the **top-level domain** (org). While there has been talk of changing these designations, the primary ones are com (commercial), edu (education), gov (government), int (international), mil (military), net (network resources), and org (nonprofit organization).

So let's say your friend tells you to send her e-mail. "My address," she says, "is Lin at coolsite dot com." Nod with confidence. When you sit down at your computer, you'll know that you need to enter "Lin@coolsite.com" (the "dot" everyone keeps talking about is just a simple period). Most e-mail systems are not capital-sensitive, but if you type "lin@coolsite.com" and your message doesn't go through, maybe the one you're dealing with is. Some systems will not send your message if you leave a space where there shouldn't be one. There are never blank spaces in an e-mail address. Most would-be blank spaces are replaced by underscores (_) or dots (.). Also be sure not to type quotation marks around an e-mail address, just the address itself.

BEFORE YOU START

Hold it just a minute. You should be completely clear on how to use your e-mail system before you sit down to compose your e-mail masterpiece and begin distributing it. The best way to accomplish this is to have a very tolerant and computer-wise friend come over to show you how to do everything you'll need to do: address your mail properly, send a message once you've written it, and access and read your incoming mail. If no such friend is available, use the Help function that comes with your e-mail program. Understand the instructions. Practice on sympathetic family and friends before torturing less accommodating e-mail acquaintances.

You're bound to make some mistakes. Not every message you send will get where it's supposed to go. Picture the post office's dead letter office. Luckily, if you make an error in addressing an e-mail message, it will come back to you. This is called a **bounce** or bounced message.

E-MAIL FEATURES

Every e-mail system is different. Your current system may or may not have some of the features discussed below, but in your e-mail life, you're bound to encounter most of them.

One of the handiest features is an **address book,** which, as it sounds, allows you to create a file of the addresses you use most. The appeal, of course, is that rather than reentering the e-mail address each time, you can just select it from your list.

There will be times when you'll want to enclose documents with your e-mail, just as you might with a snail-mail letter. There are functions for attaching other files to your e-mail message. Let's say you wrote an epic poem in honor of Bastille Day using your word-processing program. You can "attach" the poem file to an e-mail using a simple function, which is vastly easier than cutting and pasting it, or retyping it into an e-mail message. Of course, you must first be sure that your receiver's program can read your attachment.

Some systems offer return receipts, the e-mail equivalent of a real letter sent return receipt requested. This function sends a message back to the e-mail-message writer, informing him when the note has been opened. While this may sound like a groovy way of keeping tabs on the status of your mail, you should think about the implication of using this function. What signal could it send to the recipient? Perhaps he'll just think you're anal, but he may perceive it as an indication that you expect him to be pokey about responding, which, of course, would be less than flattering.

Once you've gotten past the goosey excitement of your first overstuffed e-mail box, you may realize that getting all that mail isn't as exciting as you once thought it would be. This is especially true if much of the mail is pure junk, also known as *spam*. Some e-mail programs have the ability to create a filter. A **filter** or **kill**

file is an efficient way to get rid of annoying e-mail before you even read it. You can set up your filter to automatically delete messages from those senders whose mail is always so annoying or dumb as to be unworthy of your time. Some filters can help you prioritize your mail. Instead of listing it in the order in which it was received, it will place the most important e-mail messages— let's say work-related e-mail—first, then custom-prioritize the rest of your mail.

A SUBJECT HEADING IS WORTH A THOUSAND WORDS

As an e-mail writer, you may sometimes find yourself filling in the address portion of an e-mail message box, but leaving the subject line blank. Maybe you can't think of a clever way to summarize what you've just written; they're going to read it anyway, right? Not necessarily.

A subject line is a valuable resource to those who receive a lot of e-mail. It allows them to prioritize, sort, and file messages according to subject. Not everyone can read all the mail that comes in each day. Some people use their filter mechanisms to sort their mail according to subject headings, and you're not helping them out too much by leaving it blank. Subject headings allow those who receive hundreds of messages each day to make informed choices. Guess what choice they'll make on a message marked "No Subject"?

Admittedly, subject headings are not that important when writing to your cousin or your best friend from junior high. But pretend for just a moment that you are a very popular e-mail person. Say it's late Wednesday night and you're scrolling down your list of sixty-three e-mail messages. If you see one that says "Thursday Sales Meeting Canceled," you'll probably read it. Even if the body of the message were the same, if the subject line had been blank, or had said "Update from Headquarters," you might not have read it. But come Thursday morning you'd have wished you had.

It's also a good idea to use upper/lower or all lower case when typing your subject heading. E-mail veterans know that subject headings typed in all caps are the mark of junk-mail messages; they're likely to delete such messages without even opening them.

You should also use the subject line to warn someone when your message is really long. Let's say you finally have a chance to write back to Roy about your views on McLean Stevenson's post-*M*A*S*H* endeavor, *Hello Larry*. And let's just say that it takes you two hours and twenty-five minutes to write it (which is even longer than the show was on the air). It will take Roy a long time to read it. Your subject heading should read: Hello Larry (long). Any time you send an unusually long message, include the word *long* in the subject heading.

SIGNATURES: CHOOSE YOUR HANDLE WITH CARE

A signature (or signature file or sig file) is a block of text that you can create which will appear at the end of each e-mail message you send. Not everyone chooses to have a signature; it's a matter of personal preference. Different e-mail systems have their own methods for creating signatures, and there are also self-contained programs that can create signatures for e-mail.

E-mail signatures were originally used as an easy way to pass along contact information—name, e-mail address, perhaps some professional and/or geographic information. But, as with all things out there in computerland, signatures have evolved. And as with all things, this is not always a blessing. If e-mail is the primary vehicle used to navigate cyberspace, signatures have become a form of vanity license plate. People use their signatures to pass along quotations, tidbits of bumper-sticker wisdom, and goofy ASCII diagrams that look like Etch-a-Sketch drawings.

Your signature is your little cyber-self-definition, and the way others start to define you as well, especially those who only know you through this medium. To some, this may seem like a welcome opportunity to rewrite their high school yearbook quote ("What a long, strange trip it's been" indeed). It is important when creating a signature to remember how ubiquitous it is. You had better *love* that signature.

While most people may simply ignore signatures on the e-mail messages they receive (except those with an awful lot of time), work associates may wonder why your e-mail message concludes with an Alice Cooper quote. You should never use a signature, other than one that contains contact information, in business situations.

If you do decide to use a signature, be sure to keep it brief. Signatures over four lines are considered inconsiderate, annoying, and a waste of bandwidth.

chapter seven

e-mail
etiquette

OKAY, CLASS. LET'S BEGIN.

Beginning in grade school, we all learned how to write an informal
letter ("Dear Billy, Hi. How are you? I am fine. Today I played
catch with my neighbor. Please write back soon. Your friend, Clar-
ence") and a formal letter ("Dear Mr. President: I think you are
doing a great job. Please send me a picture of you and your family.
Thank you. Sincerely yours, Garry Loomis"). Because we used to
spend the post-holiday season writing thank-you notes to aunts
and grandmothers, it is something most of us are at least mildly
adept at.

But e-mail is one of those things they threw at us later in life.
Most people don't give it a second thought, and that really shows.

E-mail is a unique medium with its own quirks, and if you want to communicate effectively in it, you have to be aware of the many nuances that are lost in cyberspace. If you take the time to think before you write, it will show and you will be admired by all those with whom you correspond electronically.

KEEP IT CLEAN

Just because you can write it in your pajamas and get nearly instantaneous responses doesn't mean e-mail is an informal, slangy mode of communication. E-mail is still written communication. That means complete sentences are required. Spelling and grammar count. Thoughts must be organized in a coherent fashion. The basic rules of English still apply, and if you didn't learn them at that uncomfortable wood desk in school, now would be a good time to retool. The format in which you write should be easy to read: Type your messages in single space and double space between paragraphs.

Say what you need to in the most direct fashion; keep your messages concise by writing short sentences and short paragraphs. There's no reason to take three paragraphs to say what can easily be written in one. While you may enjoy writing long, rambling letters, try to keep your readers' needs in mind. Some with whom you communicate may still work on *Flintstones*-era systems— reading a long diatribe on a system that clunks along is just no fun. And some users pay for the time they are online. In other words, the longer your letter, the slimmer their chances of dining out on Friday night.

RESPONSE TIME

You should expect an enormous range of response times from those with whom you correspond electronically. Not everyone is as prompt and efficient as you are.

Some people—those who are always at their computers—read their mail several times an hour. Others check theirs as infrequently as every couple of weeks. And then there are those who don't even know how to access their e-mail accounts.

Once you have a flowing correspondence with certain people, you will begin to get a sense of their individual response times. When someone's taking vastly longer than usual, a reminding nudge isn't necessarily a techno–faux pas, but keep it friendly. Instead of writing another message, you may want to nudge by phone, as the slowdown resides in e-mail. Just remember that a hallmark of the e-mail medium is convenience. Whenever possible, you should give someone at least a couple of days to respond. If your e-mail is business-related, be very specific about when you expect a response and what you expect that response to contain.

Also be mindful of your own response times. How often do you check your e-mail? If you receive work-related e-mail, you should check it daily at least, but probably more than that, depending on your average volume. Whenever possible, respond immediately, or your online in-box may start to remind you of the world's messiest desk, with unanswered letters sticking out from half-opened drawers. Once a letter has been there a while, you may never get back to it. And if you know your response will take longer than normal, dash off a short message to that effect.

It's also a good idea to read all your mail before responding. If time doesn't permit that, at least check the subjects and from whom you received mail before writing a response to anyone. You may have received more than one message from the person to whom you are responding, and she may have requested more information, or negated her previous request. To be sure that you only need to write once, review all your mail first.

On a cautionary note, it's also important to consider your response time when you are responding in anger. It's very easy to sit down and write an automatic, angry *Oh yeah?!* response, but it might be a better idea to stand up, walk around a little, and think before clicking on that Send button. Consider how you would phrase your response if you weren't separated by a network of computers: Would you rant your angry message to someone on the phone? To her face? Are you comfortable with the idea that, unlike something spoken, your e-mail message may exist on the receiver's computer forever? Think before you send; getting your e-mail back before it is read can be tough or impossible.

And from the painful but true department, there are people you write to who may just not *want* to write back to you. Say you dug up the e-mail address of that girl who was your lab partner in high school chemistry. She was really cute and funny. You write to her. No response. She may not be so thrilled to hear from you. Or you may receive a curt response: "Good to hear from you. I'm married, happy, and living in Wyoming. I hope all is well." Take the hint. Not everyone will want to be your e-mail buddy.

>QUOTE BACK

When you're writing a response to a message you have received, you may frequently go back and forth between the letter you're writing and the one you received. But you're not so likely to go back in your files to the letter before that, the one you wrote that prompted the one you received. So when you read, "In response to that weird comment on Thursday, I definitely agree," you are likely to have no idea what weird comment was made on Thursday. Or was it a comment *about* Thursday?

While we may think of e-mail as a more casual form of letter writing and more formal than phone conversation, it's fundamentally different from each of these. The lag time between sending and receiving letters can really interfere with the flow of an online conversation. That's why, as a little reminder, e-mail letters often contain quotations from previous letters. Quotes are usually indicated by the greater-than sign (>) and are kept separate from the rest of the text of the letter (usually by double-spacing).

Most e-mail programs have reply functions; many quote back the entire message. If you want to keep your friends and not anger e-mail pros, be sure not to overdue the quoting thing. Do not forward whole letters or postings unless it is entirely relevant and necessary, as it wastes time and bandwidth and makes people very cranky. Edit out the irrelevant stuff before quoting back.

WORD
WRAP

If you have ever received mail that was broken up in a really annoying way on your screen,

looking something like this, you understand the necessity

of keeping your lines

under sixty-five

characters. It is a nuisance to read a message of broken-up text

because of a

wacky word-wrap function.

Word-wrap problems frequently occur when users quote back parts of previous letters. The problem is that different e-mail programs accommodate different line lengths. So your e-mail program, which automatically inserts a return at the end of a ninety-character line, is being quoted back by a program that automatically inserts a return at the end of sixty-character line, and it never bothers to erase the old returns. Now you have twice as many returns, resulting in haiku-looking prose. Keep your lines short to begin with and you can avoid the problem completely.

DON'T WRITE JUST TO WRITE; IT AIN'T RIGHT

There are some days when your mailbox will be disappointingly empty, and you'll be tempted to write mail to generate mail. If you do this with a friend, that's fine. The whole point of a friend is she has to put up with annoying things that you do because she likes you. But don't bug your business associates if you have nothing to say. There's no need to send a colleague an e-mail message to inform him that you sent him a paper memo that should be on his desk this afternoon. If, however, you requested a response to a memo by a certain time and have not yet received it, an e-mail message reminder is perfectly acceptable.

Now, what if you are just dying to have a full mailbox each time you turn on the computer, and you receive a chain letter that promises you not only more mail, but money, too! *Do not send along a chain letter!* While you may get more mail, it will not be the kind you want to read. A more compelling argument: If it involves money, it's illegal for you to send it. If you want mail, join an unmoderated mailing list. Your box will be stuffed.

EXCUSE ME, THAT WAS PRIVATE!

Don't kid yourself. Nothing is private.

Years ago, when cutting and pasting involved scissors and sticky white stuff, forwarding messages was an involved process. Now that e-mail has made it as simple as the click of a mouse, it seems that people are quicker to share messages, including those that were intended to be kept private.

You may write something to Hank, assuming it will be read only by Hank. He may not realize that, or may not care. He may forward your message to another person, or to a mailing list. As you write, especially to people you don't know too well, assume this will happen and write with discretion. If you want to try to prevent it from happening, inform Hank that you do not want your message to be forwarded to anyone. If you want to make it even less likely to occur, consider using another form of communication, like the telephone or snail mail, to convey the information.

Conversely, respect the privacy of others. Ask permission before forwarding others' mail or portions thereof, unless it's 100 percent clear that the person who wrote the message will not mind. This rule applies even if it's good news. ("Guess what? Rosemary got that big promotion!" Rosemary may not want the world to know. She may want to tell them herself. It's not your news to tell.)

There have been occasions when people did not mean to forward a message, but have done so accidentally. That's why it's so important to be sure you know how to use your system properly. In the great big world out there, it has happened more than once that someone thought she was forwarding part of a message when in fact a whole message, or even a series of back-and forth messages, was being forwarded. And boy, was her face red.

Also, as with snail mail addresses and phone numbers, do not give out others' e-mail addresses without their permission.

USING E-MAIL TO AVOID CONFRONTATION

E-mail has replaced so much that used to be taken for granted in offices everywhere: too many memos each day, quick phone calls to arrange meetings, change-of-policy announcements. In many cases, it has also replaced the opportunity for you to look at someone's face while you speak with him.

Many people are cowards. For these chicken-hearted people, it is ever so much easier to write an e-mail message about someone's unprofessional conduct, read it over, and click a mouse to send it than to sit across a desk from that person and say those very same words to her face. But again, just because we can use the technology in this way doesn't mean we should. It's true; it is very difficult to criticize a person to her face. But it's also your responsibility when you are that person's supervisor.

If you are tempted to use e-mail in a situation like this, don't, you big sissy. With e-mail, the person to whom you are writing loses a lot of important cues and clues that he could benefit from if you were brave enough to say it to his face. He would be able to gauge from your demeanor whether or not this was a terribly big deal, for example. You owe the person a face-to-face conversation, and if it's still hard, try to remember to be careful to distinguish between criticizing the person's behavior and criticizing the person, and all that other malarkey the human resources people told you.

ARE WE FRIENDS OR BUSINESS ASSOCIATES?

Make sure you know the answer. E-mail has had the wonderful benefit of making friends of people who never had time for correspondence before, frequently people who know each other professionally.

But make sure you know which hat you're wearing when you send and receive e-mail. When you send an e-mail message about lunch next Thursday, is it to discuss the Academy Award nominations or will you be showing up with the sales department in tow? In e-mail, it is all too easy to assume your reader knows exactly where you're coming from, and that's not always a good assumption.

ONLY TO WHOM IT MAY CONCERN

Many people maintain e-mail distribution lists of people to whom they send a single message—groups of work associates, college buddies, committee members, friends with similar interests. Each time, before you send a message to an entire group, make sure it is appropriate for each person on that list. Your boss may be on your work/memo list, but if, say, you're planning a surprise party for her, or, more likely, an after-work get-together to discuss her latest act of tyranny, it's probably best that you remove her from the list. If you're going on vacation and need to inform everyone in your department, you don't need to send the message to everyone in the company. Consider all the recipients through this simple filter: Do they need the information in this message or am I just wasting their time?

This is equally important when dealing with personal messages. E-mail is not always as private as we think; you have to assume people other than the intended recipient(s) may be reading the mail you send. This is especially true if you are sending e-mail to a friend's business computer account. In other words, never send profane mail to someone's e-mail account if it is set up at their place of business. It's also not a great idea to send a message to your friend's work e-mail address if you're referring to that amazing drunken night when you did all those unspeakables. Because you never know.

SPECIAL RULES FOR HOME BUSINESSES

If you maintain a single e-mail account for both personal and home business use, remember that what is okay in an informal note to your pal may not be appropriate in business correspondence. While you do not need anything special to communicate with friends, an e-mail letterhead might be a good idea for business correspondence, but be sure to keep it brief—you don't want to waste bandwidth, for crying out loud. You simply need to convey your contact information: name, e-mail address, phone number, and address. And it bears repeating: Make sure you do not have a goofy e-mail signature, like "Jethro Tull Rocks!" going out with each business dispatch.

CHECK IT TWICE

Before long, you may grow very cocky about your e-mail abilities. It is a relatively simple way to communicate with a vast number of people. You will be pointing and clicking like you read about— reading mail one minute, forwarding messages the next. Slow down. Make it a point to always check your messages. Sure, it's simple, but some mistakes are simple to make. What if you pulled the wrong address from your address book? What if that catty letter you wrote about your old roommate finds its way onto her husband's computer? Did you address that long, informative, and overdue response to yourself by mistake? A quick check of the address and header information takes little time but can save you a great deal of embarrassment.

It's also a good habit to reread the body of your message before sending it. How does it look? Try to be objective: How would this sound if you were the recipient? Would it make you mad? E-mail is notorious for *not* conveying humor (see pp. 100). "Hey, bozo," may seem funny when you say it on the phone, but it might make your nephew cry when he reads it. Did you include references that aren't clear? A really stupid typo? It's worth the time to make sure.

If your e-mail system does not automatically copy and save

everything you send, you may want to cc yourself on important e-mail messages so you can keep a record of your electronic correspondence.

YOUR HUMOR IS LOST ON ME

A lot of misunderstandings occur in cyberspace because a lot is lost in the translation to this medium. When you're being mildly sarcastic in a face-to-face conversation, your raised eyebrows and rolling eyes give the person to whom you are speaking a good hint about how to process the words she's hearing. In a phone conversation, the way your voice rises and falls, the pauses between words, and the volume at which you speak provide clues for how the person at the other end is to interpret your message. What might seem funny on the phone may seem hostile in e-mail, as your inflection is not there to convey the humor.

Like all written communication, e-mail must fit all its information into the words on the paper or screen. If I said to you, "You looked fantastic yesterday," you could tell from looking at me whether I meant it or I was being sarcastic. (If you knew me at all, you would assume I was being sarcastic.) Even on the phone, you could draw information from my tone of voice. But your e-mail message is woefully one-dimensional. An additional problem unique to e-mail is that some of the features we commonly use for emphasis in other forms of writing—italics, underlining, bold— are not available in most e-mail programs.

Guess what? People who have been writing e-mail for a long

time have come up with emoticons, abbreviations, and other tricks to help us navigate our way through e-mail. You may or may not consider this to be a good thing. In any case, you will encounter these out there in cyberspace and you need to know what you're dealing with.

SMILE WHEN YOU SAY THAT

E-mail's infamous inability to convey subtle subtext was the impetus for some person, most likely related to the Have-A-Nice-Day smiley-face inventor of the seventies, to come up with **emoticons,** or **smileys.** Emoticons are little sideways faces which are intended to give the cues that we get when talking face-to-face but lose in e-mail. They are drawn from the regular type characters on your keyboard. It is said (by smiley users) that a good understanding and usage of emoticons can help minimize opportunities for misunderstanding.

For example, I might write to my good friend,

"I feel like killing my cat today. :)"

The little smiley face after my sentence indicates amusement—I was just joking. I would hope that she would thus understand that I was not, in fact, making plans to murder Mittens, and that she would not need to notify the local animal authorities or animal lover Bob Barker.

Emoticons are definitely an area where you don't want to overdo it. In fact, this is an area where you may not want to do it at all. While it is true that e-mail messages can be flat and do lack the visual and aural cues we get from conversation, they are not vastly different from other written communication. If a columnist wants you to know he's writing something funny, shouldn't the main clue be that it *makes you laugh*? Thankfully, you don't see little smiley faces punctuating the text in books, the newspaper, or magazines. At least not yet.

It is best to let your *writing* convey the mood or tone you wish to put forth. (And anyway, the kids who overused smiley-face stickers on their looseleafs were never popular for very long.) Just be sure that your implied sarcasm is not interpreted as meanness, and do your best to ensure that there is no room for misunderstanding.

This list of emoticons is far from complete—there are books and Internet sites devoted to smiley awareness, should you develop a serious passion for them. But try not to.

:-)	Smile	:-\	Undecided
:-D	Huge smile	:-P	Sticking out tongue
:-(	Frown	:-&	Tongue-tied
;-)	Wink	:-I	Ambivalent
:'-)	Tears	:-*)	Clowning
:-o	Surprised	%-)	Silly
>:-(	Angry	I-o	Bored
}:->	Devilish	:-c	Bummed out
O:-)	Angelic	B-)	Cool (note the sunglasses)

Another method is using brackets to indicate expressions or actions. For example, you may see the following:

[g] small grin
[G] large grin
[BEG] big evil grin
[VBG] very big grin
[hug]
<giggle>*
<groan>* (may be necessary for frequent pun-makers)
<sigh>*

Note: Some people feel that when an activity involves noise, as in a giggle, <these> are the appropriate brackets. And for a silent hug, [these] would be more appropriate. Most people, however, don't care.

There are still other ways to indicate emphasis within your e-mail messages. You can stress certain words in your messages through the use of intensifiers. Look at these examples:

"I *really* mean it."

This might look like a typo to you now, but you'll find your brain will slowly begin to accommodate this new way of communicating.

Some people may also use an underscore as an intensifier:

"I _really_ mean it."

Because underscore is also used for other functions, it's best to stick with asterisks for emphasis:

"I *really* mean it; I did love _Catcher in the Rye_."

ABBREV.

In your e-mail life, you may find yourself using the same expressions over and over. While this use of clichés would have been red-marked by your English teacher, some folks who spend a lot of time writing e-mail have found a way to make it even easier. Here's a list of commonly used abbreviations:

AAMOF–As a matter of fact

AFAIK–As far as I know

ASAP–As soon as possible

BAK–Back at keyboard

BCNU–Be seeing you

BFN/BBFN–Bye (-bye) for now

BRB–Be right back

BTW–By the way

CMIIW–Correct me if I'm wrong

F2F–Face to face

FAQ–Frequently asked questions

FOAF–Friend of a friend

FWIW–For what it's worth

FYI–For your information

GBWM–Get back with me

GD&R–Grinning, ducking, and running

GMTA–Great minds think alike

HHOK–Ha ha, only kidding

HTH–Hope this helps

IKWYM–I know what you mean

IDK–I don't know

IMHO–In my humble opinion

IMNSHO–In my not so humble opinion

IMO–In my opinion

IOW–In other words

IRL–In real life

ITRW–In the real world

IYKWIM–If you know what I mean

JMO–Just my opinion

LOL–Laughing out loud

LTNS–Long time no see

NRN–No reply necessary

OIC–Oh, I see!

OTOH–On the other hand

OTTH–On the third hand

OTTOMH–Off the top of my head

PDS–Please don't shoot

PITA–Pain in the ass

PLS–Please

PMFBI–Pardon me for butting in

PMFJI–Pardon me for jumping in

ROFL/ROTFL–Rolling on (the) floor laughing

RSN–Real soon now

RTFM–Read the [expletive deleted] manual

SHID–Slaps head in disgust
SO–Significant other
Sp?–Spelling? (you're unsure of
   the correct spelling)
THX–Thanks
TIA–Thanks in advance
TPTB–The powers that be
TTYL–Talk to you later
TTFN–Ta ta for now

TWIMC–To whom it may
   concern
UL–Urban legend
WRT–With respect to
YIU–Yes, I understand
YMMV–Your mileage may vary
   (your results may not be
   the same as mine)

chapter eight

out on the Net

how the information superhighway works

Once you know how to use your e-mail, you're ready for the world beyond friends, acquaintances, and coworkers. The fun can begin. Hooray! But first, a bit more about the technical side of things.

Your computer can communicate with systems all over the world. Let's start by considering what it means for computers to talk. There are different ways this can happen—through a local area network (LAN), a wide area network (very good—WAN!), or through phone lines. A **local area network** is one that is constrained by distance; in other words, the computers are physically connected by a cable. For example, a department of fifteen workers within a building may have a LAN, and it would run very fast. **Wide area networks** can be geographically dispersed and are usually connected over dedicated phone lines (which means not that they're loyal and won't talk behind your back, but that they're always connected). Naturally WANs run slower than LANs because of their wider range. Your computer can also communicate by using your modem and dialing directly into someone else's computer via nondedicated phone lines.

So, what is the Internet? What is the World Wide Web or Information Superhighway? People use the terms interchangeably, which is close enough to correct, but there is a small difference. The **Internet** is a huge network (that's right, a WAN— you make me so proud) of computers all over the world. Of course, not every computer is directly connected to every other computer, so if, for example, you wanted to send e-mail to another continent, your message might go through five different computers to get there.

While the Internet is the computers themselves, the actual machines, the **World Wide Web (WWW)**, which people also call the Information Superhighway, is the software aspect of the Internet. It is the method which allows you to store and access information from other computers in a very simple fashion, by following links from one site to another. Stay tuned; this will make sense.

There are different ways to access the Internet. Some institutions and businesses have direct access to the Internet, but for most this is cost-prohibitive. Most of us access the Internet through an online service or an Internet service provider (ISP). **Online services**, such as America Online (AOL) and Prodigy, provide their own newsgroups and chat rooms along with Internet access. An **Internet service provider** gives you access to the Internet and may allow you to store a web page, which we'll get to shortly.

You can also access the Internet without a computer. Web-TV is the best-known brand name for this type of technology, which basically dresses up a slightly scary piece of technology to look like a more familiar piece of technology. In other words, it's a computer in TV clothes. You buy a special box that hooks up to your phone line and television set and provides Internet access. The line on this new technology is that the television format will transform surfing the Net into a social activity, with groups of people gathered around and participating together. Maybe, maybe not. In any case, this technology appeals to some computer-phobic people by eliminating some common fears, because the only thing for which you can use it is accessing the Internet. That means no accidental deletion of your wife's really important database. Its way-lower cost is also appealing to some. The obvious downside is that your wife can't use your Web-TV to create a really important database or execute any other basic computer function; it can only be used to access the Internet.

WHAT INTRICATE WEBS WE WEAVE!

Strap yourselves in, folks, we're about to get to the beauty of the Internet. A **web *page*** is a document—viewed on your computer as a single screen. A **web*site*** is where a grouping of related web pages are located. A **home page** is the home base, or first page, of a website. All websites are different—that's the fun!—but most home pages contain a list of the material included within the site.

It's like a table of contents. Often these descriptions will contain links directly to the contents they describe. Some home pages also include links to other websites.

A **link** is what surfing is all about. It is usually displayed in a different color from the rest of the text, and is often underlined. When your cursor is over a text link—poof!—the cursor will turn into a hand with index finger pointing. If you click your mouse, it will connect you directly to another site, or page within a site, displaying an hourglass until the connection is made. In addition to taking you to other sites, links can also trigger nifty music to play, start downloading a program, and other fun stuff.

So when you're looking at a home page, rather than scroll through sections you don't want to read, you can often click and go directly to what you do want to read. If you return to the home page after following a link to a different site, you will find that the name of the site you just visited is now in a different color (unless you're working on a black-and-white screen). This handy feature helps you distinguish between sites you've visited and those you have not.

When you start exploring the Internet, you'll discover a whole world of web pages and websites. Different websites may intrigue you for different reasons. Some are the proverbial "nice place to visit"—once. Others, though, are compelling enough that you'll want to visit them again and again. To facilitate that, you can use your browser (see pp. 111) to add it to a menu you have created. The next time you want to go to that site, you won't have to surf your way in or remember the exact address; you'll just go to your "favorite places" or "bookmarked" menu, click, and be there.

THE LANGUAGE OF THE INTERNET

Hypertext is a kind of software for managing data in which you follow paths between links. **Hypertext Markup Language (HTML)** is the programming language in which web documents are created. The reason HTML it so valuable is that all computers can read it. Since it is simply ASCII text, unlike most computer programs, it is universal. HTML is most readily recognizable by its highlighted words, those links we've been talking about.

You may have wondered what that other H abbreviation is, that HTTP business that you see at the beginning of so many website addresses. **HTTP** stands for **HyperText Transfer Protocol,** the foundation of the web. It is the special protocol that's used by computers communicating, usually over the Internet.

NO, THANKS, I'M JUST BROWSING

Fortunately, groups of intelligent people have been getting together, sipping coffee, and inventing things that make it easier and more fun for us to access information on the Internet. A **browser** is a software program designed to help users view web documents. Examples of browsers are Netscape Navigator, Microsoft's Internet Explorer (IE), and Lynx. (For the most part, the only people still using Lynx are those on old clunky computers that cannot support Windows.)

For many of us, words like **File Transfer Protocol (FTP)** make our heads roll back and induce a sudden, satisfying slumber. But here goes: FTP is a protocol for transferring files, just as HTTP is a protocol for transferring web pages. In other words, it allows you to connect to other computers and either upload (transfer) files to that computer or download (transfer) files from that computer. Pip, pip, you say. Great.

Here's the nifty thing: It used to be that you had to know and understand this FTP business, because to access information you had to know the exact address or name of the computer you wanted to contact, and you had to use FTP to access the information. Now your browser is your techno-servant; it does the work. As an example, let's say you wanted to download a new tic-tac-toe game because you find them really interesting and challenging. Your browser can go to the computer where a gaggle of games are and locate the appropriate website or home page. There may be a list of games there. All you have to do is click on the link to the game you want. Your browser—without your even knowing or understanding what it's doing—will invoke the FTP program and will log you in and download the program from that computer to your computer.

While all browsers can help you navigate the Internet, their output is not necessarily the same. What you see on your Netscape browser may be different from what your friend sees on her Internet Explorer browser. The whole idea of a browser is that it *interprets* the HTML information. Think of it this way: If you gave an essay in Spanish to two different translators, you would not expect to get the exact same English version from both. There is nuance to language, similar to the kind of room for interpretation you find with HTML documents.

YOUR VERY OWN WEB PAGE

Nearly everyone with Internet access can create a web page, from the White House, to your best friend's father, to the BBC, to a guy who sells dead bugs from his basement.

At some point you may decide it's high time you had a web page so people could get to know the real cyber-you. There are plenty of sites out there to help you create one, but before you begin, you should make sure your ISP or online service provides a web-serving program (not all of them do).

People create web pages for a number of reasons—to describe themselves and their families; to discuss hobbies; to show off; as a tribute to celebrities, books, television shows, etc.; to publish stories and articles that might not find traditional publication elsewhere; and ever so many more.

The good news is that anything goes. Almost. What doesn't go is pages that take more than a minute to load. Think about the web pages you've seen. What's been really annoying? Waiting and waiting for your computer to download all the graphics? Probably. Graphics are fine, but they should be simple and must never be overdone. Remember, many people downloading your page are using slow modems. Proceed with the cyber Golden Rule—make your page as easy to use as the pages you most enjoy—and you'll have no problem figuring out what to include in your own web page.

Unless you have a very good reason not to, you should include your e-mail address and the date on which your page was last updated. If you want feedback—and you probably do—make it easy for people to reach you.

Don't have too much information on any one page. A website allows you to present a lot of information in an uncluttered, layered format. The key to keeping your website neat is to break it into multiple pages.

As for hyperlinks to other web pages, if you make a specific reference to another web page, you should include it as a link. When you do provide a link, you should also include the full Internet address, as someday, somewhere, a person may have occasion to read a hard copy of your web page, and it can be difficult to click on a link on a piece of paper. Keep in mind that you don't want to overdo the links thing. That falls into the too-much-of-a-good-thing school of website design.

If it is important to you that people visit your website frequently (if it is designed in support of a business, for example), refreshing the content often may encourage folks to return.

chapter nine

let's go Surfing now, everybody's learning how

I GOT MY BOARD, NOW WHAT DO I DO?

How will you know when you're surfing? Once you start riding those waves through cyberspace, following links from site to site, you will have joined the ranks of surfers. Say you're reading a web page about goats and you see a highlighted word or series of words leading to another web page, this one about keeping goats as pets. How lucky! That's exactly what you were looking for. You don't have to do anything complicated, like type a command to go to that web page, which is probably on a different computer network from the first one. All you have to do is point your mouse at those highlighted words—that link—and click. You will jump from one document to another. You're surfing! Surfing is basically exploring the Internet by following links. Web documents on the Internet provide the ultimate combination of cross-referencing and speed.

COME ON IN, THE WATER'S GREAT!

So you've started surfing. You should know that until you've been at it a while, you'll be considered a **newbie.** This is a widely used term to describe newcomers to the net. Though it's a sweet-sounding diminutive, it's generally not used in, oh, say the same way a mother may call her young child "pumpkin" or "sweet pea." You do not want to be labeled a newbie. Fortunately, a little knowledge can go a long way toward helping you put forth the appearance of a veteran Internet user.

The Internet is constantly evolving. As more people become comfortable using the technology, there's more to see and enjoy. Websites offer much more than information—there's a lot of interactive and entertaining stuff out there. Some sites allow you to chat with famous people. There are games to play, quizzes to take, cards to send to other Internet users. It's fun.

Many websites have **message boards**, a place where people can write and read messages on a particular subject. Some message boards offer complex search engines that let you search past messages according to various criteria, while some are simply organized by date.

In your surfing journeys, you will come across wondrous things. For example, there's free software out there! **Freeware** is software you can download and use for free. **Shareware** is also software you can download for free; however, if you use it for more than thirty days, you are obligated by law to pay a registration fee

to the author or owner. It's also known as try-before-you-buy software. Shareware and freeware are also available in many commercial outlets, but you will probably have to pay for the cost of
disk duplication.

SEND OUT A SEARCH PARTY

You're out there. You're surfing. But there's so much to see. Before
you get lost in the rising tide of overwhelming information (or in
this metaphor), grab your search engine, dude. A **search engine**
is a very handy surfing tool. These programs, like AltaVista, Yahoo, Infoseek, and Excite, allow you to search the Internet by using
keywords or combinations of keywords, or by offering you in-depth
menu systems. They are not something you even have to go out
and buy—they're already out there on the Internet just waiting
for you to come along and use them.

Search engines accomplish what you always wished your research partner would do when conducting library research. They
check everything really quickly, cross-reference, and then provide
a neat list of findings. Then, when you realize you want to focus
your research on some smaller subset, they help you with that,
too. And they never hiss "Shhhhh!"

The thing about search engines is that you have to learn how
to use them well, or else they'll drive you crazy. You may do a
search that brings up no results, or the wrong results. More likely,
your search will bring up 2,074 matches. You don't want to deal
with that. You need to limit your search, to focus it on exactly the
information you're looking for.

If you're searching with an engine like Yahoo that offers you a complex menu system, and you're able to find the right menu item, it will get you the information you want very efficiently. But if none of the menu items seem exactly right and a simple search doesn't work, you might be better off with an engine that searches on keywords. When you use keywords, with an engine like AltaVista, you need to use very specific, accurate language that describes precisely what you're looking for. You can also employ logical operators—words such as *and, not, or, near,* and *like*—to combine different words for a more focused search.

Let's say you've been contemplating losing twenty-five pounds or getting hair plugs or something, and you need some motivation, like maybe a big high school reunion. But of course you're not going to torment yourself for nothing—you need to know if your high school even *has* reunions. And let's say that rather than just calling your high school to find out, you've decided to look on the Internet, since this example won't work otherwise.

You start out using AltaVista. If you're a goofball and don't know what you're doing, you might start by just entering the keyword *reunion.* Then you would be treated to a listing of the kajillion web documents that contain the word *reunion.* That won't help you much unless you're a reunion junkie. To modify the search, you enter the name of your high school. You should put it in quotation marks, since it's more than one word: "High School of Maintenance Engineering." (Otherwise, the search engine won't know the words are to be considered together.) You add the word *and,* and the word *reunion,* and then click on search. The search engine finds all listings that contain both words. Maybe it just finds one—

the motivation you need—that announces the reunion is in seven months. And then you can start conducting a search for hair-replacement techniques and weight-loss centers.

If one search engine doesn't work well for you, try another. Different search engines may search in diverse ways and come up with varied information. Experiment and find the one that works best for you.

And don't forget that the Internet is a great way to find people, too. Rather than calling directory assistance in every area code in the country to find your long-lost best friend, you can get your hands on that information right away with an Internet search. If you don't find someone right away, don't forget that people grow up: Your good ol' fraternity brother Murph may now be going by Floyd Chandler Murphy III.

chapter ten

venturing into the Cyberworld

BULLETIN-BOARD SERVICES

Once upon a time, when an easy-access Internet was still a cybertwinkle in some figurative eye, there was something very useful called a bulletin-board service. People would use their modems to call into a particular computer that was set up to make files available and host discussion groups. For the most part, bulletin-board services—each of which was confined to one computer system accessed via direct phone calls—have been replaced by the Internet. Because nearly everyone who would want bulletin-board access already has Internet access, bulletin-board services have pretty much become a techno-relic.

MAILING LISTS AND NEWSGROUPS

When many people think of the Internet, they imagine an enchanted cyberplace where people who share their interests get together to discuss the topics their friends can't tolerate anymore. Mailing lists and newsgroups are the forums where that magic happens. Each is a cyberplace for ongoing discussion of a specific topic.

Let's look at mailing lists first. A mailing list is a group of subscribers who receive and send e-mail messages on a specific topic. The process is simple. Subscribers to a mailing list send e-mail messages to a specific e-mail address at which there is a piece of software in place called a **mail reflector,** or a **listserver.** A mail reflector sends the e-mail messages it receives to all addresses on a given mailing list (or listserver mailing list). You don't need to understand how a mail reflector works; your e-mail knowledge is all you need to navigate a mailing list. It's simply a matter of reading and sending mail, with the primary difference being that a whole posse of readers will be receiving the messages you send.

A **newsgroup** is a cyberplace where people post articles about a particular subject. Unlike a message board, which is usually part of a website, a newsgroup is a whole separate entity. The benefit of a newsgroup over a mailing list is that rather than reading through everything that has been sent to you on a given day, you can seek out articles of particular interest when you wish to. Conversely, it is not as simple as reading your mail. To read newsgroup information, you use a browser or run a special software program called a **newsreader.**

A browser or newsreader program reads article listings from a news server, which is a computer that stores articles. It is usually an Internet service provider (ISP) or a private computer on the Internet. When you post an article to a newsgroup, it goes from your computer to your news server. The news server then propagates the articles to other news servers over the Internet.

Let's look at the difference between mailing lists and newsgroups in more concrete terms. Say you're fascinated by unannounced changes of actor in prime-time television in the late sixties/early seventies and you've found a mailing list on this very subject. Now let's say you and 450 other people subscribe to it. On a given day, twenty people post messages on the topic. Those twenty messages will be sent to the e-mail boxes of all 450 subscribers. Now you want to post a thought you just had about the fine job the second Darren did replacing the first Darren on *Bewitched*. For both a mailing list and a newsgroup, it's basic netiquette (Internet etiquette) to first read what has already been posted, by looking through the group or list's archives or list of frequently asked questions (FAQs), if available. If no one else has come up with the same smashing idea as yours, you post it. If someone has, and has already made all the points you planned to make, maybe this is your chance to write up your brilliant thoughts on the two different actors who played Chris on *The Partridge Family*. In any event, once you are sure your ideas have not already been discussed, you write up your message and send it the same easy way you send e-mail to a friend. Even though you only send your message once, your ingenious thoughts will be received by all 450 subscribers.

But now pretend it's a *newsgroup* concerned with unannounced changes of actor in prime-time television in the late sixties/early seventies. You would then post your message using your news-reader or browser. But your message would *not* be sent to everyone who ever read the newsgroup. It would simply be there, ready for the user who went looking for it.

LET'S START NEAR THE VERY BEGINNING (A FAIRLY GOOD PLACE TO START)

Mailing lists and newsgroups are very easy to navigate once you know what you're doing. Usenet newsgroups, once an entity sep-arate from the Internet, are now primarily read via the Internet. There are thousands of Usenet newgroups, and their names gen-erally describe their topics of discussion. Not all ISPs and online services provide access to each newsgroup. Look over the Usenet lists of groups available to you and you are likely to find at least a few that interest you. To subscribe to a newsgroup, you simply mark the group as "subscribed" by using your newsreader/brow-ser.

You can subscribe to a mailing list by sending e-mail. Most mailing lists have a separate administrative address for requesting a subscription. Send your requests to the administrative address, which usually begins with "listserv@" or "majordomo@". The other address you will see listed is the one for posting messages. You want to be sure *not* to post your subscription request. If by mistake you do, that means everyone subscribing to a list will read your doofy message requesting a subscription. And you will quickly learn the definition of *flame*. (To learn the definition in a less painful way, keep reading.)

Once your subscription is accepted, you will receive a letter welcoming you to the list. Save this letter. It may contain useful information, such as how to unsubscribe if and when you realize that it's not actually so much fun anymore to, say, discuss the strategy of Yahtzee! in detail.

POSTING YOUR BRILLIANT IDEAS

Once you've determined that you have the right group and that your question or statement is not addressed in the list of FAQs, you just have to make sure to stay on topic. A **thread** is a subject that is being discussed in a newsgroup or mailing list—a discussion in progress. Follow a thread for a while before contributing. Just as it's more polite to join an ongoing group conversation in real life by waiting and listening to the others for a while before adding your two cents, it's nicer to follow the thread before barging in with your own opinion.

Before you post, make sure you really have something to say. The *I agree* and *good point* school of contribution is not highly respected in most online discussion groups. And you don't want to blather. A **blatherer** either likes to hear his own cybervoice or failed freshman English or both. She's someone who can go on and on without saying anything. You know, someone who would post a message like "Right on, sister," with nothing new or interesting to contribute.

If you make your way around various newsgroups and decide

that the post you've just written is not only brilliant but relevant to more than one newsgroup, it is okay to cross-post. **Cross-posting** is posting the same message to more than one group. It should not be overdone.

MODERATION OR SATURATION

There are distinctions regarding how online discussions are handled. One very significant distinction is whether or not a list or newsgroup is moderated. With unmoderated lists and newsgroups, everything sent is posted. While this may sound like a glorious celebration of freedom of speech, it can really clutter the newsgroup or your mailbox with junk. With moderated mailing lists, there's a grown-up in charge. This grown-up—the moderator—decides what will be posted and what will not. She's usually a volunteer. Going back to our example, if your prime-time TV character-replacement mailing list were a moderated one, someone would weed out inappropriate messages, such as a posting about an actor switch on a *daytime* drama or Tim Conway replacing Lyle Waggoner on *The Carol Burnett Show* (which was obviously just different).

There is another distinction regarding how messages are posted. Some mailing lists will **digest** the messages into a single e-mail file. This is true for both moderated lists and unmoderated lists. The messages will not be sorted and/or edited, but simply compiled into a single e-mail file. Digests are generally dispatched daily or weekly. To get a sense of the difference: Assume that seventy-eight messages are posted to a list in a week. With a digested list, you would receive one e-mail message that contained all seventy-eight. If it were not digested, you would receive seventy-eight individual e-mail messages in the course of that week.

CHITCHAT

A chat group or chat room is a place for real-time online discussions. Chat rooms are provided by most online services; on the Internet, chat is frequently referred to as **IRC,** which stands for **Internet Relay Chat,** a program that allows you to chat, enter chat rooms, or set up a private chat.

Chat occurs in real time, which means responses are instantaneous—online, cyperspace dialogue. Participants talk by typing their dialogue into their computers. Dialogue appears on the screens of all those involved in the chat, reading something like a script. Online services and websites provide different chat rooms based on interests, geography, age, and more, as well as general chat areas.

Many people use aliases when they're chatting. For a large number of people, the appeal of chatting online is that they can present themselves however they want to the cyber-community. But in most cases if you're chatting with an online service, your screen name is your chat name.

HOW LOVELY TO CHAT WITH YOU

The etiquette of chatting is much harder to define than e-mail etiquette, as chat rooms have a more anything-goes attitude. In fact, for many people, the main allure of a chat room is that you can shed your real identity and become some other fictional cyberperson entirely. So for those of you who are wonderful, polite Netizens, feel free to shed a degree or two of formality. But if you're a big show-off jerk in real life, it's time to learn some manners. Here are a few things to keep in mind.

Just because anything goes doesn't mean you can do something illegal, like slander someone. And remember that the person who describes herself as an eighteen-year-old go-go dancer is likely to be a fifty-eight-year-old construction worker or a seventh-grader venturing out for the first time on the Web.

Before you jump into any online discussion, you should lurk for a while. Despite the term's negative connotations, it's good to lurk before joining an online chat. **Lurking** means reading before contributing, and it ensures that you get the nature and tone of the discussion before you start blabbing.

You'll get the flow of chatting from chatting. You'll also learn from the mistakes other chatters make. As with e-mail, make sure to use your Return key to keep your lines under sixty-five characters. Do not use only upper case. It is ideal to use both upper and lower appropriately, but there's an army of users out there who think lower case only is the way to go. Don't monopolize the chats; type your messages and then allow time for others to respond. And as you would in a face-to-face or phone conversation, say good-bye, and don't disappear until the other folks have had a chance to say good-bye to you, too.

More than almost any other cyberplace, chat rooms, because

they exist in real time, rely on basic common sense. Act politely. Don't ask dumb questions on purpose because you think it's funny. (It's not.) Do not go into a chat room for orchestral musicians only to crack a series of cellist jokes. You can have fun without spoiling other people's good time. And if you type the same message over and over, which is known as **flooding,** you're ruining the fun.

WEBCASTING

By now you've figured out that the Internet is generally a passive entity. When you want information, you have to be the active one—you go out and get it. But webcasting turns that idea upside-down.

With webcasting software, such as Pointcast and Backweb, up-to-the-minute information is sent directly to you, reading like a ticker tape across your computer screen. You simply specify what information you're interested in—stock reports, weather updates, sports news—and it comes to your computer automatically. Webcasting software is available as shareware that you can download.

Netiquette

MIND YOUR MANNERS

In a simpler time not long ago, to be regarded as an upstanding member of the community you needed only to know how to engage in a hearty handshake. But by expanding the community to global proportions, the Internet has complicated the landscape. Even if you are someone who comfortably follows the Golden Rule in the regular course of your life—even if your report card said in plain black and white that you play well with others—you may find yourself at a loss out there. Rules exist for our new world. You just need to learn them.

Netiquette, as you may know, is etiquette for those interacting on the Internet. Unfortunately, you need to know more than the term. There is a plainclothes group of Internet police out there, just waiting to cuff the newbie who makes her first (and second, third, and forty-sixth) mistake out on the Net, and there are some easy ways to avoid being hit. Some of it is simple common cyber-sense, and some is specific to the Internet.

The most important rule is to be polite. Just because you are not actually talking face-to-face with these cyber-acquaintances— even though you'll probably never meet most of them—doesn't mean you have license to be rude. Just as in the real world, you have to treat your new Internet cronies with respect. If you're requesting a favor or service, say "please." Thank people who pass information your way. Once you've been out there awhile and encounter a lame newbie's mistake, remember that you were once a newbie and don't berate the poor guy.

If only everyone followed the basic rules, a lot of problems would be avoided. Unfortunately, you are likely to encounter a lot of angry people out there who are far less polite than you and I. Be cool. Remember in elementary school there were always those bad kids who'd taunt you? (Or was that just me?) Anyway, the wise adults would always tell you not to let them get a rise out of you, because that was just what they wanted. It was hard then, but it's easier now. Ignore them. They need attention; let them get it someplace else.

You know that it's rude to shout, right? BUT DID YOU KNOW THAT THIS IS CONSIDERED SHOUTING IN CYPERSPACE? If you've been out there awhile, chances are you do. You should never use all uppercase in an e-mail, a posted message, or a chat environment. If you absolutely despise the Caps Shift button, go the lowercase route, but don't be surprised if you find yourself pissing people off. Persistent whispering can be just as bad as endless shouting. It may be easier for you to write all in one case— either upper or lower—but it's not as much fun for the reader.

Be sure to lurk before you leap into the online fun. Lurking is the techno-term for playing the wallflower for a while. Let's say you just discovered a mailing list for your favorite TV show and you want to write a message saying how great you thought last week's episode was. Don't. At least not before you lurk. Lurking isn't limited to chat rooms; it's good netiquette for all online discussion. There's a strong possibility that the discussion on last week's episode is long over.

Lurking, or doing your research, ensures you don't reveal yourself as a newbie. There's no reason to contribute right away. Reading for a while before posting your first message gives you an opportunity to get the general tone and level of discussion. Many newsgroups and mailing lists have archived past discussions so that you can review them in a single sitting, getting yourself right up to speed.

There seems to be a need out there to announce one's former lurking status when posting to a newsgroup or mailing list for the first time. It's the cyber-cousin of calling in to a talk show and saying, "This is (you) from (your town), long-time listener, first-time caller." You don't need to play that card, but if you're scared of making a mistake and being found out as the newbie you are, maybe it's better to just announce it.

Perhaps even more important than lurking before posting is reading the FAQ (Frequently Asked Questions) file or document. Most mailing lists and newsgroups contain these lists of questions that kept coming up within a discussion group. The questions, and their answers, are listed by topic. It is vital that you read the FAQs before you post a question to a group. Someone took the time and trouble to compile the list so that subscribers to the mailing list/ newsgroup would not have to constantly revisit the same questions over and over.

Lurking and reading the FAQs will also ensure that you ask questions and post messages in the right place. If you've been out there awhile and participate in a number of groups, you know how annoying it can be when someone posts a question about Winnie the Pooh to your woodworking newsgroup.

SPOILER WARNINGS

You know how when you start talking about a movie with a group of your friends, someone always starts sputtering, "Don't! I haven't seen it yet! Don't ruin it." There is an Internet equivalent, known as a spoiler warning. If you are posting a message or article about some art form, such as a play, movie, or book, and you are about to refer to something that would spoil the fun for someone who hasn't read/seen/listened to it (e.g., "And then, at the end, you find out he's a woman!"), you should include a spoiler warning. A spoiler warning lets readers know that you are about to reveal something important that they may not want to know, and is generally followed by a lot of blank lines, allowing a person to get around the information without ruining the surprise.

Spoiler warnings are used whenever it would be considerate to inform certain people that they may not want to read something. As an example, within a newsgroup for victims of violent crimes, a spoiler warning could be used to advise readers that graphic content follows. While some readers might benefit from others' accounts, other readers might not feel equipped to read such things.

THE NASTINESS OUT THERE

If you've been venturing into cyberspace awhile, and have been contributing as well as accessing and retrieving information, you have found that it's not all fun and games.

Maybe you made a mistake. Heavens! Chances are more than one person let you know, and unfortunately, they probably weren't all very kind. Maybe you've been flamed. A **flame** is a nasty, insulting, confrontational message sent in e-mail or posted in a newsgroup in response to a message. It's bad netiquette to flame, but of course the word wouldn't exist if it didn't happen. You should not be flamed for making a mistake, for your opinion, for posting a question that's covered in the FAQs, for bad grammar, or just for being alive, but you may be. Try not to flame at all. If you come across something that is clearly wrong and in need of correction, correct the error in as polite a way as possible.

If you are going to flame someone in a chat room, which is a terribly rude thing to do, at least make sure you do it in the most polite way possible. By beginning with "FLAME ON" before the flame message, and concluding with "FLAME OFF," you will at least let readers know what to expect. And if you must flame some-one publicly, like to a whole mailing list, inform them of your intention in your subject heading so those who like to avoid con-frontation can. (Of course, it would be less cruel just to send your rude message directly to the person's e-mail box, but flamers are not known as manner mavens.)

On the other side of the flame coin: If a flame brought a legit-imate mistake to your attention, you may want to apologize, if appropriate. Nothing wrong with that. Just make sure you don't get defensive when you say you're sorry. And keep it brief.

Maybe you have noticed that there are some people whose post-ings are simply unbearable to read. Sometimes they post messages on subjects that really rankle people (such as fanatical nationalist or religious messages) in inappropriate places. Unfortunately, these are the people who seem to have the most time to post. These annoying posts are often put out there as **flame bait** (a message intended to inflame readers). People, can't we all just get along? The only thing to do with this is ignore it.

SPAM, SPAM, SPAM

But how do I ignore all the spam, you may ask? Or perhaps you're asking what *is* spam? **Spamming** is sending vastly inappropriate messages or junk e-mail to a newsgroup or mailing list. (Not inappropriate as in slightly-off-the-subject-in-a-newsgroup, but more along the lines of get-rich-quick/pyramid schemes.)

There are ways to deal with spam. The best way is not to deal with it. If you're not overwhelmed by the amount of spam you receive, just delete each message. Do not respond to it and do not forward it to someone else. Some companies that have ongoing, wide-ranging spam problems on their e-mail systems set up special security accounts that try to track down the culprit computer or computers and cut it/them off from further communication. If yours does, forward spam to the security account.

And make sure you're not part of the problem. You get a letter from your old friend Lyle, who apologizes but says he's sort of superstitious and he couldn't help sending along this chain letter. What you do is your business, Lyle says, but he couldn't keep himself from passing it along. Go for it, he urges; you can make a wish when you continue the chain. Do not listen. Never pass along a chain letter. You had an excuse when you were in elementary school and believed that bad things would happen to you if you broke the chain. But you're a grown-up now. Behave like one. Just say no to junk mail.

If you need more help dealing with your spam, it's out there. The beauty of technology is that there are so many smart people trying to solve problems as they arise. Some software programs offer a feature that helps weed out spam. By employing a **mail filter,** this function trashes the messages from known spam violators before you even read them. Some programs even have a tattle-tale function that automatically sends a message to the system administrator from which the message originated, and reports the behavior of the spam-monger using their service. Justice, at last.

TAKING IT TO E-MAIL

Remember this one? There is a time and a place for everything. Much of what goes on in the public's view—in mailing list discussions, within newsgroups—would be better served in the relative privacy of e-mail. When you're in the midst of a newsgroup discussion that has gotten into a detailed study of minutiae that is interesting only to you and one other person on earth (who happens also to be part of the newsgroup), it is time to take it to e-mail. That means instead of posting your response for the whole group to endure, you and your boring little friend should have a private e-mail discussion (by sending messages directly to each other's e-mail address).

A series of back-and-forth flames, or a **flame war,** should also be taken to e-mail. Unfortunately, for many flame baiters, the whole fun of the fight is the public spectacle.

Likewise, you should never post a personal message to a newsgroup or mailing list. "Hey, Bruce. Want to meet before the show?" Not okay. Even though participants in some mailing lists develop cyberfriendships and cybercliques, it is a medium for group discussion. Everything posted should be of relevance to all involved.

Play It Safe in Cyberspace

THE POLITICS OF PASSWORDS

It's really important, and that's why everyone keeps repeating it: Don't tell anyone your password. And don't have an obvious, goofy password like your name or anniversary or child's birthday. What is the best password? Unfortunately, it's usually one that's hard to remember. That's because instead of it being something oh-so-clever like drowssap, a good password will combine upper and lower case, numbers, punctuation, and letters.

There's a bit of password etiquette you should be mindful of, too. When you're at someone's computer and she's entering her password, look away. Sure, you and I know that you would never use her password for evil purposes, but how is she supposed to know that?

USE YOUR NOODLE

E-mail is not as secure as snail mail. It is best to assume that anything you send via your computer is *not* secure, unless you are employing encryption software (the techno-equivalent of a secret decoder ring). Encryption translates a message into a coded message that your receiver's browser will know how to decode. You should not generally include your credit card number in e-mail correspondence; it's just too risky and there are other ways to provide the information that are not as likely to end up damaging your credit history. It is safe, for example, to send your credit card number using a browser if it employs a "secure" method. (Use the Help function of your browser to figure out the specifics of this one for your particular browser.)

THE INTERNET AND CHILDREN

There are many situations in which parents have no choice but to send their children into the world; they cross their fingers and hope for the best. When it comes to children using the Internet, that isn't good enough.

It's just like the real world. There are lots of wonderful things out there, but there's also some stuff that makes us shudder. A great deal is entertaining, informative, educational. Some is violent and sexual and vile. Children, even older children, cannot be counted on to stay away from the bad stuff.

Parents need to play a supervisory role in their children's online adventures. Fortunately, there are endless resources available to parents that help them to do precisely that. Your online service or ISP may have an option that restricts Internet access by blocking addresses of inappropriate sites. There are online groups. There is software. School districts form committees to address the issue. There are endless books. Get involved.

If you feel as if it's too late, that your kid is already out there, and you, until recently, thought the mouse was a foot pedal, that's a cop-out. Let your child show you what he knows. Ask him to give you a tour of the Internet. And once you know your way around, set up strict rules. Your child must know that he should never give out personal information online. Do not permit an unaccompanied child to meet someone in person he has met previously only through the Internet; it's great to make friends through e-mail, but a person isn't always who he seems to be. Anything your child receives that seems inappropriate should be brought to your attention. You should then notify the online service or Internet service provider.

As parents you have to become informed, be vigilant, and only then cross your fingers and hope for the best.

chapter eleven

when to do  What

WHAT ARE YOUR OPTIONS?

Now you know how to do everything in the communications world, and how to do it with finesse. Bravo. But there are so many means available to us to communicate with one another; how do you know *when* to do *what*? Unfortunately, there are no hard-and-fast rules. But you can make an informed decision.

Let's look at the possibilities. You can call someone on the phone, send a fax, beep them, call their cellular phone, send them e-mail, or send regular mail. There are other things you could do, too—such as video conferencing—but we could be here all day, for crying out loud.

The best way to use these technologies properly is to understand the owner's preferences and to make your own preferences known. When someone gives you all their techno-vitals—address, phone number, fax number, e-mail address, beeper number, cellular phone number—they should also advise you of their preferred order of communication. If they don't offer up their wishes when they give you the information, it is perfectly polite—in fact, savvy—to ask. Likewise, when you give out your various numbers and addresses, let the person to whom you are giving them know your own personal techno–rock, paper, scissors. "Try me at the office first. If I'm not there, you can always send me e-mail; I read it at least three times a day. If it's an emergency, call my assistant; he'll know how to reach me. If you absolutely must, try me at home, but never after seven." It's also a good idea to define what an emergency is. To some, it's "I couldn't find the office copy of *People* magazine." The best way to ensure people are respectful of your technology wishes is to educate them and to make wise decisions: If you don't want anyone but your family to call you on your cellular phone, don't give out the number.

And don't assume everyone has access to the same technologies as you do. Presume nothing. Instead of asking for someone's e-mail address, it's much more polite to ask if she has an e-mail address. Likewise, fax number, cellular phone number, beeper number, etc. There's still a whole world of people out there who rely primarily on a telephone.

PROS AND CONS OF POST AND CALLS

If you've called Steve's office and left a message, and you have Steve's beeper and cellular phone numbers, what are you to do?

It depends. Chances are if Steve gave you his beeper number he is telling you that you should feel free to use it. Unless he said otherwise. This is why it is so important to find out a person's preferences *before* you get into a situation where you wish you had already asked.

When you call someone's beeper, as with leaving a message, you are efficiently tossing the responsibility into their court. It's nice to have it not be *your* problem anymore, but it doesn't really solve anything if what you really need is to speak to the person immediately. With someone who uses her beeper efficiently, maybe you'll get a call back quickly. That would be nice. Problem solved. Unfortunately, a person can't always get to a telephone immediately. And then we're back to the position of trying to co-ordinate the schedules of two busy people so they can both be doing the same thing—talking on the phone—at the same time. If a person does not call you quickly after you beep her, the chances for eventual contact are generally far lower than those you'd have with a message left with an assistant or on a machine. People seem unusually comfortable forgetting or ignoring their beeper messages. And don't forget that sometimes people really don't receive their pages—if they're out of range, you're out of luck.

As for cellular phones, the rules still vary. For many people, they are part of everyday communication, but for others, it's still a guarded, emergency territory. A safe rule to follow is if someone gave you his number and said nothing about it being for emergency use only, you should feel free to call him on his cellular phone.

When possible, choose regular phone over cellular phone—because in general, regular phone is the cheaper choice.

If you and the person you're trying to contact have access to e-mail, you can send some. Good idea. But what if the person you're writing to only checks her messages once a week? Or usually checks every day, but forgot today? Or is diligent, except the machines are down? If you have an existing e-mail relationship with the person, you can call and notify him that you've sent him a message.

It's a similar situation with a fax. Have you ever walked into an office and seen papers littering the ground below a fax machine? Not every office has an efficient fax-delivery system in place. And for those people with fax machines in their home or home offices, the machines could be in the attic for all you know. It offers pretty good speed—put it in the machine, transmit, *voilà!*—but there's a definite lack of accountability. How many times have people told you they never got your fax? How many times have you lied and said you never received a fax that you did in fact receive, just to buy yourself some time? It's too easy.

If you have tried to reach someone through more than one medium, it's a good idea to inform the person of such. Otherwise, you may get an e-mail message, phone call, and fax in response to what was only a simple question. Something like this is fine on someone's voice mail: "Hi, Derek, it's Jane from RCI. I sent you an e-mail message and a fax yesterday. I need to speak to you before tomorrow's meeting. Please call me at . . ."

Most of the messages you leave or send will probably not require confidentiality. You should, however, be mindful that each technology offers a different level of security. E-mail and cellular phones offer you the least security, whereas snail mail offers you the most. If you are discussing important spy secrets or other information that needs to be kept extremely discreet, take that into account before you choose your communication method.

FORMAL OR CASUAL?

One of the benefits of technology is that it makes communication so simple. One of its greatest faults, too, is that it makes communication so simple. Something is lost.

Remember when you were seven and the mail came and there was something for you? Wasn't that exciting? Remember when it was an invitation to that bowling party that all the hip second-graders were going to? There was something satisfying about holding it in your hand, then tearing open the protective envelope and revealing its precious contents.

And what of the long-lost art of thank-you notes? Think of what you've received in the last year that could be described as thank-you communication. A phone call saying, "Hey, great party." An e-mail message saying, "I appreciate the business." Handwritten thank-you notes are disappearing.

Formality goes a long way. It takes more effort to sit down and handwrite a thank-you note, address an envelope, place a stamp on it, and get it into the hands of the U.S. Post Office. But the reward is great; the effort does not go unnoticed. The same is true for invitations. A different mood is created depending on the form of invitation. A phone call may mean an informal dinner party whereas a written invitation creates a different level of expectation. An e-mail message could be best suited for an after-work get-together. Consider the level of formality you wish to convey, and don't overlook the one that takes the most effort, lazybones. People appreciate that effort.

As for the big question of the day—is it okay to fax or e-mail a thank-you note or other personal correspondence? Not usually, but sometimes. Here's the deal: If you *know* in your heart of hearts that you will *never* get around to sitting down and writing out a note, but at this moment, right now, you have five minutes to write a really quick e-mail, it is definitely better than nothing. (This is your politeness conscience speaking: The truth is, you could take that five minutes and handwrite one, place it in an envelope with a stamp, and mail it.) Here's your rule of thumb: The only time it's okay to fax or e-mail a thank-you note is if you will never express thanks in any other way.

When choosing the right medium, it's a good idea to stop for a minute and use your brain. We're so accustomed to just *doing* that we frequently fail to envision the end result. If you stopped to *think* about it, you would never send a message of condolence via e-mail or fax, right?

There's a definite modern tendency to use the fastest means available even when it's not necessary. Have you noticed how many letters and packages are sent by overnight carriers? People do this simply because they can. But for small companies and home offices, the cost of overnight mail may be a significant one that cannot be assumed to be standard operating procedure. It is good form, when you expect people to respond via the method you prefer, to send along a prepaid self-addressed overnight envelope, especially in those instances in which you are responsible for the need to rush (as in "Didn't start the assignment a month ago, but waited until Monday, even though it's due Thursday").

While the fact that you have more choices does make things more complicated, it has also vastly improved your life. Technology can affect and improve relationships. So many people are too busy to keep up with old friends. A technology like e-mail allows friends who would probably never write and mail each other letters to carry on simple epistolary correspondence. And for those who maybe think too slowly for the telephone, e-mail permits the immediacy of contact without forcing their brains into unnaturally high rpms.

chapter twelve

traveling with technology

BEFORE YOU TRAVEL

When was the last time you lost a valuable computer file that was difficult to recreate? Remember that feeling? Before you and your laptop go out on the town, make sure all important documents have been backed up. Even if you manage to hold on to your laptop, it is more likely to be broken in transit than it is sitting on your desk, and you'll want to be sure you have copies of important files. Now that I have your attention, why not just back up *everything* you have on your computer, laptop or otherwise?

And while you're at it, how about bringing along the phone number for your cellular carrier? If you run into problems, you'll be glad you have it—especially if the phone gets stolen.

EQUIPMENT FOR YOUR EQUIPMENT

There are lots of different carrying cases out there designed to protect your laptop computer and your cellular phone. But you know what else they do? Advertise to potential thieves that you're carrying a laptop and cellular phone. Remember those news stories about people who worked in teams, stealing laptops at airport security sites by creating a diversion right when the unsuspecting victim's laptop rolled out on the other side of the carry-on luggage conveyer belt? Not only were they true, but they gave a whole bunch of less creative thieves a good idea, making this an even bigger problem.

It's true that your laptop needs to travel in comfort—something that will prevent it from bouncing around unprotected. But the best defense is not one of those high-priced rugged leather carrying cases that scream "LAPTOP." Instead, you can spend a few bucks on a laptop pouch that will keep your laptop in a closed, protected, padded compartment. And then you can carry your laptop pouch in another bag—a knapsack or briefcase—so the world is none the wiser about its existence.

Likewise with your cellular phone. There are specially designed carriers for cellular phones that you can carry on a belt or with a shoulder strap. Many include a compartment for storing an extra battery, which is a great idea. There's nothing wrong with wanting to protect your cellular phone, but there's no reason to call attention to it either. Tuck the carrier into something less conspicuous.

IN THE CAR

It bears repeating that while you can use all your swell mobile equipment in your car, you should not do so while it's moving if you're the one who's responsible for the moving. If you're a passenger, great! Enjoy! Get lots done!

You know how careful you are about hiding the cassettes and/or CDs in your car whenever you park it? Cassettes and CDs cost less than fifteen bucks, and the stereos you play them on are a couple of hundred, a smashed window a little more than that. Think about the cost of your laptop and the value of the data on it, and the potential disaster of someone using your phone to patch up a long-ago relationship with someone who now lives in Turkey. Leaving telltale signs of your technology on the passenger seat is a really bad idea. Take a look around before you leave the car. Do you have an adapter cord plugged into your lighter? Use your brain and hide your stuff.

IN THE AIRPORT

When you're in the airport, the best place to use your fancy-schmancy equipment is in one of those executive/frequent flyer airline clubs. Most provide places to hook up your computer and allow you to transmit faxes. Because it is set up for executive use, it is a perfectly proper place to talk on the phone, cellular or otherwise. On the other hand, chatting on your cellular phone in the boarding area is boorish. If you need to talk on the phone, you should find a private place.

What about all those hoops you have to jump through before you board your plane? The X-ray machines—that conveyer belt on which you place your carry-on before entering the boarding area—is not considered to be harmful to your equipment in most countries, including the United States and Canada. On the other hand, the metal detectors you walk through on your way to your gate emit a magnetic pulse that can be harmful to computer equipment. Make sure your laptop doesn't pass through that detector, and do not carry an important floppy disk on your person when you pass through.

Your laptop's battery should be fully charged before you head to the airport. Of course, it will need to be charged to allow you to work on the plane. But you may also be required to start up the computer as you go through the preboarding security clearance, just to prove it's not a bomb in disguise.

IN THE SKY

Just because many planes have phones available doesn't mean you have to use them. Again, the action itself is just plain (plane?) impolite. Sure, it's helpful when your roommate is picking you up at the airport and your flight has been rerouted to another city. But is it necessary to call your assistant again to make sure you really didn't get any messages the whole time you were gone? When seated in your crowded airplane row, you are about as physically close to strangers as you are apt to get outside of a rush-hour subway. The people next to you, behind you, and in front of you will hear everything you say, whether they want to or not. Consider that before you call to say, "Hey! I'm calling from a plane! Isn't that cool?" If that doesn't sway you, consider the fact that a ten-minute phone call is likely to cost you the same as a really good meal for two. If you must call, try to find a row of seats that is not occupied, or if the phone is cordless, take it to the back of the plane or another less crowded area.

There are some things you should keep in mind when using your laptop in-flight. If you're one of those banging typists and the person next to you is trying to sleep, let's just say she's not likely to offer to share her peanuts with you. If you use the tray table on the back of the seat in front of you, try not to rattle the person in that seat each time you cut and paste. And be sure to turn the volume off so as not to disturb other passengers.

You should also be mindful of how long your laptop's battery's charge will last and, if you travel often, consider an additional portable battery. If you need to prolong the battery's life on a trip, or anytime, you can turn down the brightness on your screen or even have your screen use the black-and-white mode to save some power.

chapter thirteen

Techno-Favors

KNOW THE RULES

It's not getting any simpler. Used to be two friends went out, bought lunch, split the bill. No problem. Now one of them asks to use the other's cellular phone, and since she forgot her wallet, she was wondering if she could just put the theater tickets she's buying on her friend's credit card and she'll pay her back.

This needs to be said and heeded: Think about all the associated costs when you're requesting a techno-favor. Rules really do change and if you're not paying attention, you can behave inconsiderately without even knowing it. Learn how things work before you ask to borrow them. With a cellular phone, for example, not only is the person *placing* a call to a cell phone charged for the call, but the person *receiving* a call on a cell phone is charged for air time. Consider that before giving your new boyfriend's cell-phone number to your chatty friend in case she feels like talking while you and your boyfriend are away camping.

And what of having your friends charge something for you on their credit cards? Of course you know that you should not borrow money you will be unable to pay back. But if everyone played by that rule, lots of people who work at collection agencies would be out of work. If you ask a friend to put something on his credit card, don't assume the ball is in his court. You're the one who needed the favor, so you are the one who must take the initiative for repayment. Ideally, you should pay him back before the bill even comes, but if you do, make sure you take into account the unseen charges. If you bought a $60 sweater, did you pay tax on it? If you purchased theater tickets that cost $65 each, was there also a $7 ticket charge and $4 order charge and $5 processing charge? You must pay back the entire amount. If you do not know the exact cost because of the possibility of unforeseen charges such as these, you can ask him to notify you as soon as the bill arrives. And then you must give him the money immediately, and offer to write the check directly to the credit card company. Have I made myself clear?

And another thing: When asking someone to "make you a copy" (whether it's audiotape, videotape, floppy disk, or whatever), it's a nice gesture to provide—or at least return or replace—the blank.

BORROWING EQUIPMENT

One of the most commonplace assumptions within the world of techno-etiquette goes some like this: Because it would be easier for you than for me to accomplish this techno-task, you should do it for me.

Figuring out when it is appropriate to ask to borrow technology is the uncharted territory of the electronic age. At one time, many offices were considered a free-for-all; people would meter their personal mail at the company's expense and photocopy résumés for friends. Now most businesses pay closer attention and run a tighter ship. And technology has permeated our lives to such a degree that these questions are not confined to the work arena; they come up at the diner, too.

Asking to borrow telephones is very different in various situations. If you are visiting a client's office, it shouldn't be a big deal; it's just part of basic business courtesy. But in most social situations, asking to use someone's cellular phone is outside the realm of polite behavior.

Let's say the copier repair guy is in your office servicing the machine again. He realizes he needs to call his office to have someone bring over a part. Not a big deal—he can be shown to a phone that is not being used. Now let's say the copier repair guy is sitting next to you at the company softball game and spots your cellular phone in your bag. It's a whole different can of worms, ladies and gentlemen.

Because of the associated costs, cellular phones have a whole other set of rules. While they may be a prevalent technology, they can still cost a lot to use, and it's presumptuous to ask. Of course, as with all situations, it's different when there is an emergency. But if you're on the soccer field and Billy just missed a goal by an inch and the woman next to you wants to call Billy's grandparents in Naples to tell them, that's just not okay. She can wait until she gets home.

There will be people who ask to borrow your cellular phone for nonemergency calls. What can you do? They're putting you in an unfair position and you have every right to do what you need to do to get out of the situation. Lying might work. Or you could mention how high your bill was last month. At the very least, ask them to keep it brief. And if you are the one asking to use someone's cellular phone, make sure you have good reason. Offer to reimburse the person for the call, and assure the phone's owner that you will keep it brief, and then be sure you do.

Now let's say you're hosting a party and inviting a bunch of big shots, some who are in the habit of forwarding their calls to the location of their social events. (Why would you want to invite these people to your party, anyway?) If you don't want this to happen, say so at the outset. The best way to do this politely would not be to mention their annoying habit but to describe the atmosphere you hope to create. Really, you are helping them to not be the rude clods they've been in the past.

There can be a slightly greater tolerance for improper techno-etiquette in some business situations, when everyone is armed with similar technologies. It is not uncommon for one business-person to ask to borrow another's cellular phone. What is more unusual, and also a bit more polite, is to ask to borrow someone's cellular phone *battery*, rather than the whole phone. If you were prepared, though, you would have had an extra charged battery and could have avoided the whole situation.

Because, for the most part, offices continue to be better equipped than the average home, there are technological tasks that can be readily accomplished there that can save someone a lot of time. For example, you work at home and your wife works in an office. You have written a screenplay that you want to mail to your cousin in California. Your wife can copy and mail it easily at the office, whereas you'd have to make two trips—one to the copy shop, one to the post office. Hmm. You know what? It's sort of like stealing. But it's done. If your wife doesn't mind, and her company is loose as a goose about such things, maybe there's no harm done. Would your wife's employer care if he caught your wife at the copy machine collating the pages of your opus? Be forewarned that people have been fired for less.

Now let's say it's not your wife, but your best friend, Terry. We're getting into riskier water here. As you know, you can ask your spouse or equivalent to do things that you can't ask anyone else to do. Maybe Terry doesn't feel comfortable saying no. (You *know* your spouse feels comfortable saying no.) Why are you willing to inconvenience Terry but not yourself? True, the technology is there, in Terry's office. But that's not why it's there. Just go to the copy shop, you slothful slug.

And while you're there, make sure you send that fax, too, because it's not nice to send Terry to the office with a résumé for him to fax out to those three places that seem so promising. If you can do it yourself, even if it's inconvenient, do it. Just because it doesn't cost Terry money doesn't mean it's free. The paper used in a copier, as well as the ink and other supplies, is paid for with real money. And the telephone connection required when transmitting a fax is charged to the sender's phone bill.

What about borrowing people's computers? That is going to depend entirely on the person whose computer you are asking to borrow. Some people take better care of their computers than they do of their children. If you do plan to go to someone's house to use her computer, and you know you'll be printing out a ton of résumés, bring your own paper. If you'll be at it awhile, offer to replace the print cartridge. And be sure you know your company's take on using your work computer for personal use, even after hours. For many companies it's no big deal, but for some, it's a capital offense.

chapter fourteen

how to be polite in a  Rude World

(A FREE-FOR-ALL LOOK AT THE NEW DEMANDS OF MODERN LIFE)

MUSIC THAT MOVES (WITH) US

There's a big difference between boom boxes and personal portable stereos. While they both help us tune out the outside world to some extent, personal portable stereos do so in the less impolite way.

If you have a boom box and you use it in public, you probably don't much care about the etiquette of it. There is no etiquette for it, because it's inappropriate to do. Boom boxes belong in your basement or backyard.

As for personal stereos with headphones, if it helps you get through your day, good. Wear it wherever you want: the subway, the sidewalk, on the beach. But don't be an idiot. Don't wear headphones while you're operating machinery, driving a car, riding a bicycle. You need to be able to hear when you're active; limiting the outside noise you hear may put your life and others' in danger. Of course, you shouldn't have your headphones on in an environment in which you are going to interact with other people. That would be a bit rude, don't you think?

You might also consider investing in larger, padded headphones—the cheaper varieties often "leak" sound and become irritating to others. And please . . . no singing along!

HANDHELD ELECTRONIC GAMES

You know the kind I mean, with the annoying, high-pitched beeps and crash sounds and bad tinny music. This is mostly a kid-etiquette problem. Here's the thing. Many of these gadgets have a little headphone adapter, and headphones should always be used outside the home. Those without headphones should be used with the volume off outside the home. Some parents swear these toys are the only way to get from point A to point B in the car without the kids killing each other. Good. There are few among us who are not all for children staying alive. Let them play. But you—and others—may go crazy from the noise if you're lax on the headphone usage/volume issue.

THINGS THAT GO BEEP IN THE NIGHT

Cellular phones and pagers are not the only annoying things that beep in the night and day. Say you're at the theater. Your watch should not beep every half hour. Your voice organizer should not alert you with a series of beeps that it's time to call the baby-sitter. Turn off such features before venturing into social situations, or better yet, leave the equipment at home.

Not everything that beeps has to beep. Picture a big meeting in a conference room. Lots of discussion. A beeper going off would be disruptive; it should be on vibration mode. Always. No alarms of any sort should go off. Even those who use laptops should make an effort to keep it quiet, which means not only turning the volume off, but also typing as quietly as possible.

ATM (AVERT, THEN MOVE)

People are using their bank debit cards everywhere now. What etiquette used to be required only at the bank is now needed at the gas station, the supermarket, and other stores. There are two main rules when using an automatic teller machine: Avert, then move.

It's basic password etiquette: Look away when someone enters her password. When you're waiting for your turn at an ATM, this means keep a certain distance between yourself and the person presently conducting a transaction. There's a sociological study that needs to be done regarding various societies' customary ATM space; what's true in the city is different in the suburbs and rural areas. When in doubt about the proper distance, err on the side of too much. And in grocery stores, which were not designed for this technology (remember when you used to pay by cash or check?) you may have to afford this distance in other ways, for example by averting your eyes.

When it's your turn at an ATM, conduct your business quickly, then move away from the machine. Unless there is no one waiting to use the machine, you should move along before entering the transaction in your checkbook. No one should have to wait while you do that. It's the real-world equivalent of waiting until you get off the green to enter your score on the scorecard.

Can you *ever* ask to borrow someone's ATM card without risking serious offense? Probably not. There was an ATM-related life-threatening emergency dramatized on *Seinfeld* . . . but in real life, don't even think about it.

SAVING MARRIAGES BY REMOTE

There was a time when people had to stand up and walk to their televisions to change channels. People didn't think this was a big deal at the time, because they were still impressed by the great picture these newfangled radios showed on their screens. But as technology improved, people got lazier and fatter and had more reason to have snitty little fights with their spouses and others about the remote control.

Some people cannot stand to watch commercials. These people feel a need to see what else may be on during commercial breaks from the shows they're watching. (These are usually the same people who have Call Waiting—those who always think something better is out there.) Unfortunately, there is no clearly defined etiquette between spouses or other significant television-watching others for who controls the remote. There is, however, a rule you can cling to when others are visiting to watch television with you. It is not okay for guests to assume control of a remote control. Never ever, unless you have graciously offered them the privilege.

I TOLD YOU TO SAY CHEESE!

The rule of thumb for all picture-taking is that you must ask your subjects first. There are people who hate to have their picture taken, hate to have their voices recorded, and hate to be videotaped. Just because you're, say, getting married doesn't mean they have to overcome their hatred of videos and come up with clever banter for the guy in the bad suit holding the camera. People should be asked before they become subjects of any picture—and this also holds true when photographing strangers. Some find it very disconcerting to have their picture taken by someone they don't know.

Here's the one that gets a lot of people into trouble: videotaping children's performances. It's understandable that you want a record of Ahmed's acting debut, portraying an acorn in the second-grade play. But your big head and camera should not be blocking the view of the non-videotaping parent sitting behind you. She should not be forced to crane her neck and practically crawl onto her neighbor's lap for a view of her daughter, the red autumn leaf. If a video record of a performance is important to you, ask in advance for permission to videotape the dress rehearsal or to find a special place to stand or sit during the actual performance. It's much more considerate.

One last video-related item: Be kind—rewind. Before you return that rented videotape, would it kill you to double-check that it's rewound? There's nothing quite like popping in the tape you reserved three weeks ago only to view the unexpected plot twist that shocked viewers worldwide in the final ten minutes of the film.

KNOW HOW TO WORK IT

You have to know the proper way to use your stuff. Sure, this has always been true, but now, because we have more stuff, it's even more true. The stakes are higher. Fifteen years ago, the most significant techno-mistake you were apt to make was setting your clock back instead of ahead for Daylight Savings Time, making you two hours late for brunch the next morning.

Now let's say, as an example, you just installed a high-tech security system. It turns your lights on for you at a certain time, sounds alarms, whatever. And let's say you didn't really pay attention when it was installed, because you knew how to turn it on and off and that was all you cared about. What happens when you lose power and it comes back on in the middle of the night? There's a good chance alarms will sound, making sure your neighbors have an opportunity to think about you at 4 A.M. This could still happen even if you *did* listen when it was installed, but at least you'd know how to reprogram the thing, and those bells could stop ringing and that voice could stop saying, "The door is ajar."

It's tempting to start up that new toy as soon as you get it, without reading the two-hundred-page manual. But don't.

keep it Legal

IT'S MINE AND YOU CAN'T SEE IT

Your e-mail is your personal business, don't you think? No one in your office, for example, should ever be poking around your e-mail account, or listening in on your phone calls, right?

Depends. If you're an employer, for example, the legal precedent indicates that you cannot eavesdrop on phone calls for kicks, but you can if you have reason to believe the conversations may be about ways to damage your company. Believe it or not, though, the situation is vastly different when the medium is different. Employers *are* in their legal rights to read employees' e-mail messages—that is, those on the company's computer system—just for fun. Look at it this way: The company *is* paying for the e-mail provider. In the eyes of the law, that may mean workplace e-mail is fair game. In fact, a company can legally fire an employee because of the content of an e-mail message she writes. It has happened.

State legislatures are expected to be charged with the responsibility of creating more up-to-date laws to govern online technology.

BUT, OFFICER, I DIDN'T KNOW...

If you break a rule of etiquette, you may be mocked by your peers mercilessly. But if you break a law, you can be judged by a jury of your peers and fined lots of money. And when they say ignorance is no excuse, they mean it.

There are loads of laws governing the things we do online every day, and most of us don't know a hill of beans about any of them. There are books on the subject and websites devoted to changes in cyberlaws that govern us all. It is your responsibility to keep yourself up-to-date.

Start thinking in legal terms. Before you copy something to include on your web page, think about it. Is it legal to copy it? If you're not sure, don't do it. If you really want to do it, find out if it's legal. You should be able to find someone in cyberspace who can answer your legal questions.

PUBLIC DOMAIN/SHMUBLIC SHMOMAIN

One way people justify their copyright-law-bashing behavior is by claiming that that to which they are helping themselves is public domain, which means it was never copyrighted, or that its copy-right has expired. Sometimes this is true, but it's not a safe as-sumption. If something *is* public domain, you can copy it, use it, or do whatever you want with it.

Copyright law is complex and the Information Superhighway has helped make it easier for us to break the law regularly without even thinking about it. But it's not a good idea. Did you know that something does not need to show that cute little c in a circle to have a copyright? As soon as something is written, it is considered copyrighted under federal law. You don't need to fill out forms or register anything to obtain that copyright.

If you want to help yourself to something that you know *is* copy-righted, you may be able to do so legally, but you have to ask permission of the person who holds the copyright. It takes more time, but it's legal. It is ever so much easier to be lazy than to be vigilant about copyright law. But a law is a law is a law.

Be careful out there.

Glossary

analog
An electronic signal that is defined by waves of widely varying amplitude and frequency.

anonymous call rejection
A telephone service that rejects calls from phones that block identifying information.

ASCII text
American Standard Code for Information Interchange, i.e., type characters without the fancy stuff. Those letters, numbers, punctuation, and characters that are available on a typical typewriter.

back up
Copy data from your computer to a storage device, such as a floppy disk.

bandwidth
The amount of data that can be transmitted over a medium in a given amount of time. Most frequent usage: "Don't waste my bandwidth," the cyberspace equivalent of "You're wasting my time," or "Stop breathing my air." Used in a sentence by someone nice: "My modem can support a maximum bandwidth of 33.6 kilobits per second."

baud rate

The rate at which data is transferred, most frequently used when discussing the speed of a modem, measured in bits or kilobits per second.

beeper

A small device designed to receive short messages of numbers or text sent by placing a phone call to a paging terminal.

bit

The smallest unit of digital information, represented by a 0 or 1.

blather

Netiquette terminology for going on and on without saying anything.

bookmark

A way of storing the addresses of your favorite websites on your Navigator browser for easy access.

bounce

An e-mail message that informs you that an e-mail message you tried to send was not delivered, usually because of a mistake in the address.

browser

A software program used to view documents on the World Wide Web.

byte

A series of eight bits.

cache

A place for storing data on a computer.

Hardware cache is comprised of chips and is the fastest and most expensive short-term memory in a computer.

Software cache is where data is temporarily stored by a program.

Call Answering

A telephone service, similar to voice mail, that allows callers to leave a message when you are on another call or cannot answer the phone.

Call Return (*69)

A telephone service that allows your phone to dial back the phone that called yours most recently.

Call Waiting

A telephone service that allows you to receive a call when you are talking to someone on the phone.

Caller I.D.

A telephone service that displays information about a caller on a screen.

CD-ROM

Compact Disc-Read-Only Memory, computer hardware that reads compact disks.

central processing unit (CPU)

The main component of a computer, which executes the instructions of the programs you run.

chat room

A virtual place where people communicate in real time by text or, in some cases, by audio.

coaxial cable

A copper wire used as a transmission line, traditionally used to transmit signals for television.

compact disc (CD)

Computer data storage medium based on optics.

conference call

A phone service that allows three or more parties to participate on a single phone call simultaneously.

cross-posting

Sending the same message to several newsgroups or mailing lists.

cyberspace

An ephemeral "place" that is not a physical location, but exists in the network of the Internet.

digest

Compilation of all mailing-list posts into a single e-mail file.

digital

Defined by series of 0s and 1s, the way computers store and process data.

digital versatile disk (DVD)

Computer data storage medium with greater capacity than CDs, designed to store video and audio.

domain name

The name given to a computer or network of computers, part of an e-mail address.

dot

The period in an e-mail address.

download

Receive information from another computer via a network or phone line.

e-mail

Electronic mail, a message typed into one computer and sent electronically to another.

emoticon

Little sideways face drawn from the regular type characters on every keyboard, used in e-mail messages to provide contextual clues.

encryption software

A tool that translates your e-mail message into a code that can only be read by the intended recipient of your e-mail.

FAQ

Frequently asked question, most commonly used to describe a list of FAQs maintained by most newsgroups and mailing lists.

favorite place
A way of storing the addresses of your favorite websites on your Explorer browser for easy access.

fax (facsimile) machine
A device that translates printed pages into and from signals that can be sent over a telephone line.

fiber-optic cable
A cable that consists of transparent materials, such as glass or plastic fibers, that transmit light and carry more information faster than coaxial cable lines.

filter
A software program that sorts e-mail according to criteria you establish.

flame
A mean-spirited e-mail message sent to inform someone that they are wrong, dumb, or otherwise at fault.

flame bait
A message intended to anger the receiver/reader and prompt a flame in return.

floppy disk
A small, removable magnetic storage medium that holds computer data.

freeware
Software that you can download from the Internet or a bulletin-board system and use for free.

FTP (file transfer protocol)
A method for transferring files between computers.

hard copy
A printed version of a computer document.

hard disk
A magnetic disk that serves as a computer's primary storage device, also referred to as a "hard drive."

HFC (hybrid fiber coax)
A combination of fiber-optic and coaxial cable lines.

home page
The root web page of a website, often like a table of contents.

HTML (Hypertext Markup Language)
A computer language used to create documents on the World Wide Web.

HTTP (Hypertext Transfer Protocol)
The protocol for transferring files, usually on the World Wide Web.

hyperlinks
A simple method of connecting one hypertext document to another.

Internet
A vast network of computers that uses specific protocols for transferring data, frequently referred to as the *Information Superhighway* and *World Wide Web*.

Internet service provider (ISP)
An organization that provides connections to the Internet.

IRC
Internet Relay Chat, a program that allows people to talk on the Internet in real time.

ISDN line
Integrated Services Digital Network, a digital network that utilizes regular telephone wires, used for higher-speed computer network connections.

killfile
A filtering mechanism that automatically eliminates mail from various sources.

LAN
Local area network, a network of computers in a small geographic location, usually less than a mile and frequently within the same building.

laptop
A small, self-contained portable computer.

link
Addresses included in hypertext documents that allow you to move to other documents by clicking on highlighted text.

log off
Terminate a connection to a computer.

log on
Establish a connection to a computer.

lurking
Reading in a newsgroup, mailing list, or chat room before posting.

mailing list
A grouping of e-mail addresses, often used to describe a service that forwards messages to a group of e-mail addresses or subscribers.

mail reflector
A software program that distributes e-mail messages to a mailing list.

message-delivery service
A telephone service, for which the caller is charged, that allows a caller to leave a message when no person or machine answers the number he is calling.

modem
A device that translates digital information from a computer to analog data that can be sent over a phone line and vice versa.

netiquette
Etiquette for communicating on the Internet.

newbie
A newcomer to the Internet.

newsgroup

A cyperplace where people post articles of interest on a particular subject.

newsreader

A software program needed to read what is posted in newsgroups.

news server

A computer that stores newsgroup articles.

online service

An organization, such as America Online, that provides Internet access and other services, such as online reservations, chat rooms, and game rooms.

pager

(See beeper.)

password

A unique identifying code that gives you access to a service such as a computer account.

per-call blocking

A telephone service, accessed on a call-by-call basis, that conceals identifying information and blocks call return from those you call.

per-line blocking

A telephone service that conceals identifying information and blocks call return each time you place a call.

personal digital assistant (PDA)

A small computer that fits in the palm of your hand, most frequently used to store personal information such as phone numbers and appointments.

personal identification number (PIN)

Like a password, a unique identifying code used to access such technology as cellular phones and automatic teller machines (ATMs).

post

Write and send a message to a newsgroup or mailing list.

POTS

Plain old telephone service, traditional analog phone lines.

public domain

Something that does not have a current copyright is said to be in the public domain.

RAM (random access memory)

Computer hardware memory that can be read from and written to repeatedly but is lost when computer is turned off.

real time

Where sender and receiver communicate immediately, without lag time.

scanner

A device that translates a printed page document with words and/or pictures into digital computer data.

search engine
A software program used to search a network of computers, most commonly the Internet, for specific information.

shareware
Software that you can download from the Internet or a bulletin-board system for free but must pay the author for if you continue to use it.

signature
Text that is appended to e-mail and news messages, usually providing personal information such as name and address.

smiley
Little sideways face drawn from the regular type characters on every keyboard, used in e-mail messages to provide contextual clues.

snail mail
Mail sent via the United States Postal Service.

spam
A message posted inappropriately to newsgroups, mailing lists, or all over the Internet.

spoiler warning
Lets online readers know that you are about to reveal something important (generally about a movie, book, play, etc.) that they may not want to know, usually followed by blank lines.

sub-notebook
A very little portable computer, even smaller than a laptop.

tape drive

Computer storage device that can hold a vast amount of data, less expensive but slower than a Zip drive.

telemarketer

Someone who calls you with information you did not request or to sell you something you expressed no interest in buying.

thread

A topic of discussion within a newsgroup or mailing list, usually identified in the subject line.

upload

Send information to another computer via a network or phone lines.

Usenet

A large collection of newsgroups.

user name

A name that identifies you to a computer.

virus

A malicious program intended to corrupt your software.

voice mail

A telephone service that answers calls and delivers messages.

WAN

Wide area network, a network of computers not confined by geographic space, generally connected by phone lines.

web page
> An HTML document on the Internet that can be read by a browser.

website
> The location of related web pages.

WINTEL
> A computer with an Intel processor and Microsoft Windows operating system.

World Wide Web (WWW)
> Often used interchangeably with the term *Internet*, the WWW is an information system that provides easy access to data on a worldwide basis.

WYSIWYG
> What you see is what you get.

Zip drive
> Computer storage device that can hold a vast amount of data, more expensive and faster than a tape drive.

Afterword

Now that you've studied up and become a real techno-whiz, there's just one more point of etiquette to master.

Remember when you didn't know all this stuff? Remember when people would ask, "What's your fax number?" as if *everyone* who's *anyone* naturally owned a fax machine? Remember how they'd huff with annoyance, "When are you going to get an answering machine/get online/get a beeper, already?" Remember how they'd snicker as you fumbled with a speaker phone for the first time, or laugh as you crouched in terror when that little picture of a bomb showed up on your computer screen?

The lesson to be learned is: be nice to newbies. We were all newbies once. And when the next wave of techno-innovation sweeps the world—any minute now—we will be newbies once again.